WHAT'S COOKING

Fish & Seafood

Carol Tennant

This is a Parragon Book
First printed in 2000

Parragon
Queen Street House
4 Queen Street
Bath BA1 1HE, UK

ISBN: 0-75253-518-8 (Hardback)
ISBN: 0-75254-034-3 (Paperback)

Printed in Singapore

ACKNOWLEDGMENTS

Editorial Consultant: Felicity Jackson
Editor: Susanna Tee
Photography: Colin Bowling,Paul Forrester and Stephen Brayne
Home Economists and Stylists: David Morgan, Mandy Phipps and Gina Steer
All props supplied by Barbara Stewart at Surfaces.

NOTE

Cup measurements in this book are for American cups. Tablespoons are assumed to be 15ml. Unless otherwise stated, milk is assumed to be full fat, eggs are medium and pepper is freshly ground black pepper.

Recipes using uncooked eggs should be avoided by infants, the elderly, pregnant women and anyone suffering from an illness

Contents

Introduction

Seafood rightly deserves its image as a healthy food. It is high in protein and with the added bonus of oily fish, such as mackerel and herring, being high in polyunsaturated fat – this is the one that helps reduce cholesterol levels. White fish are a good source of minerals as well as being low in fat, especially if poached, steamed or lightly grilled. Although shellfish have been linked with high cholesterol, they are also low in saturated fats and are therefore fine eaten in moderation.

The sheer variety of fish and shellfish is staggering. If you decided to eat seafood just once a week, you could go for a whole year without eating the same dish twice. Seafood is also quick and easy to prepare, making it an attractive ingredient to the busy cook. Often sold ready-to-cook fish can be prepared in minutes and most shellfish is sold already cooked, needing even less preparation. Fish is also very good value for money compared to meat, as there is much less waste and no fat or gristle to contend with. Therefore making fish a regular part of your diet makes a lot of sense.

BUYING FISH AND SHELLFISH

Wherever you are shopping for fish, at your local trusted fishmonger or supermarket, the guidelines are the same:

- The eyes of the fish should be clear, bright and moist. Fish with dull, grey or cloudy eyes should be avoided.

- The gills of the fish should be bright red or pink, not dull and grey.

- The fish should smell of the sea and nothing else.

- If you press the fish lightly with your thumb, the flesh should spring back, leaving little or no imprint.

- The shells of hinged shellfish, such as oysters, mussels and clams, should be tightly closed prior to cooking. If they are slightly open, tap them sharply. If they do not close, discard them.

- Cooked shellfish should smell fresh, with no hint of ammonia. If available, check the use-by-date.

STORING

As you never know how long ago the fish was caught, especially in a supermarket, it is best to buy fish and cook it on the same day. Unfortunately, modern refrigerators are not ideal places to store fish as they tend to have a temperature of about 5°C/38°F and fish is best kept at 0°C/32°F. If you have to keep fish, don't keep it for more than one or two days. Put the fish into a plastic container and scatter over some ice. Cover with cling film (plastic wrap) and keep in the coldest part of the refrigerator.

Firmer fleshed fish, such as turbot, Dover sole and monkfish, freeze better than less firm-fleshed fish like bass, lemon sole and plaice but all will deteriorate over a relatively short period. Oily fish is the least successful when frozen. However, if you have to keep your fish for more than a day or two, then freezing is the best option. Ensure that you thaw fish thoroughly and slowly before cooking.

PREPARATION

How much preparation your fish needs depends on where you buy it. Supermarkets may have a wet fish counter with a trained fishmonger on hand while others sell their fish vacuum-packed. Many fish are sold already scaled and gutted, and are often available either whole or filleted. It is usually cheaper, however, to buy a whole fish and prepare it yourself. A fishmonger will usually do this job for you for the price of a whole fish. However, it is not difficult to do yourself and only takes some practice.

EQUIPMENT

Although, in general, you don't need a great deal of specialist equipment, there are a few items you might consider if you plan on cooking a lot of fish. If, for example, you are planning on poaching whole fish, then a wise investment would be a fish kettle. This is an oblong stainless steel pan with a lifter and lid. They usually come in several sizes.

A wok or large, heavy-based frying pan is useful for frying and stir-frying. If you like to steam fish you might like to consider a double boiler, bamboo steamer or electric steamer . A thermometer is useful for deep-frying as is a deep-frying basket and large pan.

If you intend cleaning your own fish, a good filleting knife is a must. Tweezers are also useful for removing small bones.

COOKING METHODS:

Different fish suit different cooking methods but, as a general rule, poaching, steaming and stewing tend to produce moister results than grilling, baking or barbecuing. Drying out can be minimised, however, if the latter three methods are used at sufficiently high temperatures to reduce moisture loss by cooking the fish very quickly.

POACHING

The fish is immersed in a poaching liquid, which might be a court-bouillon, fish stock, milk, beer or cider. Bring the liquid to the boil and as soon as it boils, remove the pan from the heat and leave the fish to finish cooking in the residual heat. This method helps to prevent overcooking and is also excellent if you want to serve the fish cold.

STEAMING

Both fish and shellfish benefit from being steamed. Again, a flavoured liquid can be used for the steaming, which will impart some of its flavour to the fish as it is being cooked. This method is especially good for keeping the fish moist and the flavour delicate. Steaming can be done in a fish kettle, double boiler or steamer inserted over a pan of boiling water.

STEWING

Either whole fish or smaller pieces can be cooked in liquid along with other ingredients, such as vegetables, as a stew. The fish flavours the liquid as it cooks, giving a distinctive flavour.

GRILLING

This is one of the quickest and easiest cooking methods for fish. Cook either whole fish, steaks or fillets. Shellfish can also be grilled, but may need halving lengthways first. Whatever you are cooking, ensure that the grill is on its highest setting and that the fish is cooked as close to the heat source as possible. A barbecue is also a very useful tool for grilling fish. Brush the fish with butter, oil or a marinade before and during cooking to ensure that the flesh remains moist.

BAKING AND ROASTING

This covers all methods of cooking in the oven, including open roasting, casseroling or en papillote. This is a good method to choose for entertaining because, once the dish is in the oven, you are free to attend to other things.

DEEP-FRYING

The fish is either coated in batter, flour or breadcrumbs and deep fried in oil. You need a large, heavy-based saucepan or a deep fat fryer. Large pieces of fish in batter are best cooked at a lower temperature of 180°C/350°F which allows the fish to cook without burning the batter. Smaller pieces of fish, like goujons in breadcrumbs, should be cooked at a higher temperature of 190°C/375°F. Drain deep-fried items well on paper towel to ensure that they remain crisp.

SHALLOW OR PAN-FRYING

This is a quick method for cooking fish and shellfish and can take as little as 3–4 minutes. A shallow layer of oil or butter and oil is heated in a frying pan, the fish added and cooked until just tender and lightly browned. A good non-stick frying pan is an essential piece of equipment.

The argument for increasing the amount of fish and seafood in our diets is compelling. Fish and seafood can provide variety, versatility, creativity and luxury as well as being much more healthy than meat. Why not give it a try?

Starters & Appetizers

The dishes in this chapter are designed either to whet the appetite for the main course to come, without being filling, or as nibbles to serve with drinks. Fish and seafood make excellent starters as they are full of flavour and can be turned into a variety of delicious dishes. Fish is also much lighter than meat and therefore won't be overly filling.

Fish cooks quickly, making it ideal for entertaining. Many of the dishes in this chapter can be prepared in advance and served cold, such as the Anchovy Bites, the Smoked Mackerel Pâtè and the Lime & Basil Cured Salmon, or simply reheated, like the Curried Mussel Tartlets or the Stuffed Squid.

There is also a good selection of first course options, for example the Thai Crab Omelette, Potted Shrimps and Maryland Crab Cakes with Basil & Tomato Dressing, and lots of lovely salad ideas, including the Smoked Haddock Salad and the Bruschetta with Anchoiade, Mixed Tomatoes & Mozzarella.

Anchovy Bites

These delicious pastry pinwheels are perfect for serving with drinks before dinner. If you prefer, use a ready-made anchovy paste, such as Gentleman's Relish, to save time.

Makes: about 30

INGREDIENTS

- 175 g/6 oz/1½ cups plain (all purpose) flour
- 80 g/3 oz/6 tbsp butter, cut into small pieces
- 4 tbsp freshly grated Parmesan cheese
- 3 tbsp Dijon mustard
- salt and pepper

ANCHOIADE:

- 2 x 50 g/1¾ oz cans anchovy fillets in olive oil, drained
- 100 ml/3½ fl oz/scant/½ cup milk
- 2 garlic cloves, roughly chopped
- 1 tbsp roughly chopped fresh flat-leaf parsley
- 1 tbsp roughly chopped fresh basil
- 1 tbsp lemon juice
- 25 g/1 oz/2 tbsp blanched almonds, toasted and roughly chopped
- 4 tbsp olive oil

1 To make the pastry, sift the flour into a large bowl and add the butter. Rub together until the mixture resembles breadcrumbs. Stir in half the Parmesan cheese and salt. Add enough cold water (about 3 tablespoons) to form a firm dough. Knead briefly, wrap in cling film (plastic wrap) and refrigerate for 30 minutes.

2 Meanwhile, make the anchoaiade. Put the drained anchovies into a small bowl and pour over the milk to cover. Leave to soak for 10 minutes. Drain the anchovies and pat dry on paper towels. Discard the milk.

3 Roughly chop the anchovies and put into a food processor or blender with the garlic, parsley, basil, lemon juice, almonds and 2 tablespoons of the oil. Blend until smooth. Scrape out of the food processor or blender and stir in the remaining olive oil and pepper to taste. Set aside.

4 Remove the pastry from the refrigerator and roll out very thinly to a large rectangle measuring 55 x 37.5 cm/20 x 15 inches. Spread thinly with 2 tbsp of the anchoiade and the Dijon mustard. Sprinkle over the remaining Parmesan cheese and some black pepper.

5 Starting from a long edge, roll up tightly then slice crossways into 1 cm/½ in thick slices. Arrange cut side up and well spaced on a non-stick baking sheet (cookie sheet).

6 Place in a preheated oven at 200°C/400°F/Gas Mark 6 for 20 minutes until golden. Cool on a wire rack.

3

6

Bruschetta with Anchoiade, Mixed Tomatoes & Mozzarella

This colourful salad is full of flavour and textures. I have suggested mixed cherry tomatoes and beefsteak or plum tomatoes but the salad will work equally well with whatever ripe tomatoes are available.

Serves 4

INGREDIENTS

2 x 150 g/5½ oz balls buffalo Mozzarella, drained
115 g/4 oz/1 cup orange cherry tomatoes
115 g/4 oz/1 cup red cherry tomatoes
2 ripe plum or red beefsteak tomatoes
2 ripe orange or yellow beefsteak tomatoes
4 tbsp extra-virgin olive oil, plus extra for drizzling
1 tbsp balsamic vinegar
8 thick slices ciabatta or other rustic country bread
1 garlic clove
4 tbsp anchoiade (see Anchovy Bites, page 8)
handful basil leaves
salt and pepper

1 Slice the Mozzarella balls into thick slices. Set aside. Halve the cherry tomatoes and thickly slice the plum and beefsteak tomatoes.

2 To make the dressing, whisk together the olive oil, balsamic vinegar and seasoning.

3 Toast the bread on both sides then rub one side with the garlic clove. Drizzle with a little olive oil. Spread the anchoiade on the toasts.

4 To assemble the salad, arrange the sliced tomatoes on each of 4 serving plates and scatter with cherry tomatoes.

5 Top the toasts with the mozzarella slices and 2–3 halved cherry tomatoes. Cook under a preheated grill (broiler) for 3–4 minutes until softened. Drizzle over the dressing and scatter with basil leaves and black pepper.

6 Put 2 slices of toast on the plates.

Bagna Cauda with Crudités

Translated literally, Bagna Cauda means 'hot bath'. This is a typical dish from Piedmont in Italy, where it is always eaten by large groups gathered around the table.

Serves 8

INGREDIENTS

- 1 yellow pepper
- 3 sticks celery
- 2 carrots
- ½ cauliflower
- 115 g/4 oz/½ cup mushrooms
- 1 bulb fennel
- 1 bunch spring onions (green onions)
- 2 beetroot, cooked and peeled
- 8 radishes
- 225 g/8 oz/1 cup boiled new potatoes
- 225 ml/8 fl oz/1 cup olive oil (not extra-virgin)
- 5 garlic cloves, crushed
- 50 g/1¾ oz can anchovies in oil, drained and chopped
- 115 g/4 oz/8 tbsp butter
- Italian bread, to serve

1 Prepare the vegetables. Deseed and slice the pepper thickly. Cut the celery into 7.5 cm/ 3 inch lengths. Cut the carrots into batons. Score the mushrooms as in the photograph. Separate the cauliflower into florets. Cut the fennel in half lengthways then cut each half into 4 lengthways. Trim the spring onions. Cut the beetroot into eighths. Trim the radishes. Cut the potatoes in half, if large. Arrange the prepared vegetables on a large serving platter.

2 Heat the oil very gently in a saucepan. Add the garlic and anchovies and cook very gently, stirring, until the anchovies have dissolved. Take care not to brown or burn the garlic.

3 Add the butter and as soon as it has melted, serve straight away with the selection of crudités and plenty of bread.

COOK'S TIP

If you have one, a fondue set is perfect for serving this dish as the sauce can be kept hot at the table.

Giant Garlic Prawns

In Spain, giant garlic prawns are cooked in small half-glazed earthenware dishes called cazuela. The prawns arrive sizzling at your table, with plenty of local bread to mop up the delicious juices.

Serves 4

INGREDIENTS

120 ml/4 fl oz/1 cup olive oil
4 garlic cloves, finely chopped
2 hot red chillies, deseeded and finely chopped
450 g/1 lb cooked king prawns (jumbo shrimp)
2 tbsp chopped fresh flat-leaf parsley
salt and pepper
crusty bread, to serve
lemon wedges, to garnish

1 Heat the oil in a large frying pan (skillet) over a low heat. Add the garlic and chillies and cook for 1–2 minutes until softened but not coloured.

2 Add the prawns and stir-fry for 2–3 minutes until heated through and coated in the oil and garlic mixture. Remove from the heat.

3 Add the parsley and stir well to mix. Season to taste.

4 Divide the prawns and garlicky oil between warmed serving dishes and serve with lots of crusty bread. Garnish with lemon wedges.

COOK'S TIP

If you can get hold of raw prawns, cook them as above but increase the cooking time to 5–6 minutes until the prawns are cooked through and turn bright pink.

Mini Prawn Spring Rolls

These delicious little spring rolls are perfect as part of a selection of canapés. Serve with a selection of dips, as suggested in the recipe.

Makes about 30

INGREDIENTS

- 50 g/1¼ oz/½ cup dried rice vermicelli
- 1 carrot, cut into matchsticks
- 50 g/1¾ oz/¼ cup mangetout (snow peas), shredded thinly lengthways
- 3 spring onions (scallions), finely chopped
- 100 g/3½ oz/1 cup cooked peeled prawns (shrimp)
- 2 garlic cloves, crushed
- 1 tsp sesame oil
- 2 tbsp light soy sauce
- 1 tsp chilli sauce
- 200 g/7 oz filo pastry, cut into 15 cm/6 inch squares
- 1 egg white, beaten
- vegetable oil, for deep-frying
- dark soy sauce, sweet chilli sauce or sweet and sour dipping sauce (see Thai Fish Cakes, page 40, for dipping

1 Cook the rice vermicelli according to the packet instructions. Drain thoroughly. Roughly chop and set aside. Bring a pan of salted water to the boil and blanch the carrot and mangetout (snow peas) for 1 minute. Drain and refresh under cold water. Drain again and pat dry on paper towels. Mix together with the noodles and add the spring onions (scallions), prawns, garlic, sesame oil, soy sauce and chilli sauce. Set aside.

2 Fold the filo pastry squares in half diagonally to form triangles. Lay a triangle on the work surface, with the fold facing you, and place a spoonful of the mixture in the centre. Roll over the wrapper to enclose the filling, then bring over the corners to enclose the ends of the roll. Brush the point of the spring roll furthest from you with a little beaten egg white and continue rolling to seal. Continue with the remaining filo triangles to make about 30 spring rolls.

3 Fill a deep fat fryer or saucepan about a third full with vegetable oil and heat to 190°C/375°F or until a cube of bread browns in 30 seconds. Fry the spring rolls, 4 or 5 at a time, for 1–2 minutes or until golden and crisp. Drain on paper towels. Fry the remaining spring rolls in batches.

4 Serve hot with dark soy sauce, sweet chilli sauce or sweet and sour sauce for dipping.

Prawn Satay

It is well worth seeking a supplier of Thai ingredients, such as lemon grass and lime leaves, as they add such distinctive flavours for which there are no real substitutes.

Serves 4

INGREDIENTS

12 peeled raw king prawns (jumbo shrimp)

MARINADE:
1 tsp ground coriander
1 tsp ground cumin
2 tbsp light soy sauce
4 tbsp vegetable oil
1 tbsp curry powder
1 tbsp ground turmeric
120 ml/4 fl oz/½ cup coconut milk
3 tbsp sugar

PEANUT SAUCE:
2 tbsp vegetable oil
3 garlic cloves, crushed
1 tbsp red curry paste (see Red Prawn Curry, page 102)
120 ml/4 fl oz/½ cup coconut milk
225 ml/8 fl oz/1 cup fish or chicken stock
1 tbsp sugar
1 tsp salt
1 tbsp lemon juice
4 tbsp unsalted roasted peanuts, finely chopped
4 tbsp dried breadcrumbs

1 Slit the prawns down their backs and remove the black vein, if any. Set aside. Mix together the marinade ingredients and add the prawns. Mix together well, cover and set aside for at least 8 hours or overnight.

2 To make the peanut sauce, heat the oil in a large frying pan until very hot. Add the garlic and fry until just starting to colour. Add the curry paste and mix together well, cooking for a further 30 seconds. Add the coconut milk, stock, sugar, salt and lemon juice and stir well. Boil for 1–2 minutes, stirring constantly. Add the peanuts and breadcrumbs and mix together well. Pour the sauce into a bowl and set aside.

3 Using 4 skewers, thread 3 prawns on to each. Cook under a preheated hot grill (broiler) or on the barbecue for 3–4 minutes on each side until just cooked through. Serve immediately with the peanut sauce.

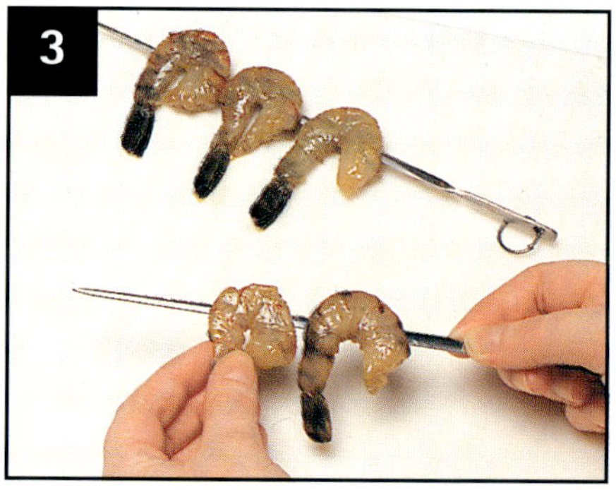

Potted Shrimps

These little pots of shrimps in spicy butter are a classic English dish, originating from Morecambe Bay in Lancashire, where they are still made to this day.

Serves 4

INGREDIENTS

225 g/8 oz/1¼ cups unsalted butter
400 g/14 oz brown shrimps in their shells or 225 g/8 oz cooked peeled prawns (shrimp)
pinch cayenne pepper
½ tsp ground mace
1 garlic clove, crushed
1 tbsp chopped fresh parsley
salt and pepper
brown bread, to serve
lemon wedges and fresh parsely sprigs, to garnish

1 Heat the butter in a small saucepan until melted and foaming. Set aside for 10 minutes or until the butter separates. Carefully skim off the clear yellow liquid and discard the white milk solids. The clear yellow oil remaining is clarified butter.

2 Peel the shrimps, discarding the shells. Heat 2 tablespoons of the clarified butter in a frying pan (skillet) and add the shrimps. Stir in the cayenne, mace and garlic. Increase the heat and stir-fry for 30 seconds until very hot. Remove from the heat, stir in the parsley and season.

3 Divide the shrimps between 4 small ramekins, pressing down with the back of a spoon. Pour over the remaining clarified butter to cover. Refrigerate until the butter has set.

4 Remove the ramekins from the refrigerator 30 minutes before serving to allow the butter to soften. Toast the brown bread and serve with the shrimps, garnished with lemon wedges and fresh parsley sprigs if liked.

COOK'S TIP

The most authentic shrimps to use for this recipe are the tiny brown shrimp. They have a full flavour and soak up the butter well. If your fishmonger can't supply them, substitute the pink peeled variety.

1

2

3

Prunes Stuffed with Mussels

This is a variation on the classic 'Devils on Horseback' – oysters wrapped in bacon. This version uses freshly steamed mussels, stuffed inside marinated prunes, which are then wrapped in smoky bacon and grilled with a sticky glaze.

Makes 24

INGREDIENTS

3 tbsp port
1 tbsp clear honey
2 cloves garlic, crushed
24 large stoned prunes
24 live mussels
12 rashers smoked streaky bacon
salt and pepper

1 Mix together the port, honey and garlic then season. Put the prunes into a small bowl and pour over the port mixture. Cover and leave to marinate for at least 4 hours and preferably overnight.

2 Next day, clean the mussels by scrubbing or scraping the shells and pulling out any beards. Put the mussels in a large saucepan with just the water that clings to their shells. Cook, covered, over a high heat for 3–4 minutes until all the mussels have opened. Discard any mussels that remain closed.

3 Drain the mussels, reserving the cooking liquid. Allow to cool then remove the mussels from their shells.

4 Using the back of a knife, stretch the bacon rashers then cut in half widthways. Lift the prunes from their marinade, reserving any that remains.

5 Stuff each prune with a mussel then wrap with a piece of bacon. Secure with a cocktail stick. Repeat to make 24.

6 In a saucepan, simmer together the mussel cooking liquid and remaining marinade until reduced and syrupy. Brush the stuffed prunes with this mixture. Place under a preheated hot grill (broiler) and cook for 3–4 minutes each side, turning regularly and brushing with the marinade, until the bacon is crisp and golden. Serve while still hot.

VARIATION

As an alternative to smoked bacon use pancetta or Parma ham, cut into strips, instead and cook as above.

3

4

5

Mussel Fritters

If you find making mayonnaise difficult, or if you don't like to eat raw eggs, use a good quality ready made mayonnaise and mix in the garlic and herbs.

Serves 4–6

INGREDIENTS

175 g/6 oz/1½ cups plain (all purpose) flour
pinch of salt
1 egg
225 ml/8 fl oz/1 cup lager
900 g/2 lb live mussels
vegetable oil, for deep-frying

GARLIC AND HERB MAYONNAISE:
1 egg yolk
1 tsp Dijon mustard
1 tsp white wine vinegar
2 garlic cloves, crushed
2 tbsp chopped fresh mixed herbs, such as parsley, chives, basil, thyme
225 ml/8 fl oz/1 cup olive oil
salt and pepper

TO GARNISH:
lemon slices
fresh parsley

1 To make the batter, put the flour into the bowl with a pinch of salt. Add the egg and half the lager and whisk until smooth. Gradually add the remaining lager, whisking until smooth. Set aside for 30 minutes.

2 Clean the mussels by scrubbing or scraping the shells and pulling out any beards that are attached to them. Discard any with broken shells or any that refuse to close when tapped. Put the mussels into a large pan with just the water on their shells and cook, covered, over a high heat for 3–4 minutes, shaking the pan occasionally, until all the mussels have opened. Discard any mussels that remain closed. Drain and set aside until cool enough to handle, then remove the mussels from their shells.

3 To make the garlic and herb mayonnaise, in a food processor or blender, whisk together the egg yolk, mustard, vinegar, garlic, herbs and seasoning until frothy. Keep the machine running, and add the olive oil, drop by drop to begin with, until the mixture begins to thicken. Continue adding the oil in a steady stream. Season and add a little hot water if the mixture seems too thick. Set aside.

4 Meanwhile, fill a deep saucepan about a third full with vegetable oil and heat to 190°C/375°F or until a cube of bread browns in 30 seconds. Drop the mussels, a few at a time, into the batter and lift out with a slotted spoon. Drop into the hot oil and cook for 1–2 minutes until the batter is crisp and golden. Drain on paper towels. Serve hot with the garlic and herb mayonnaise garnished with lemon slices.

Mussels with Pesto

These delicious morsels make an impressive, yet quick, starter. Serve them with some crusty bread to mop up any juices.

Serves 4

INGREDIENTS

900g/2 lb live mussels
6 tbsp chopped fresh basil
2 garlic cloves, crushed
1 tbsp pine kernels (nuts), toasted
2 tbsp freshly grated Parmesan cheese
100 ml/3½ fl oz/scant ½ cup olive oil
115 g/4 oz/2 cups fresh white breadcrumbs
salt and pepper

TO GARNISH:
basil leaves
tomato slices

1 Clean the mussels by scrubbing or scraping the shells and pulling out any beards that are attached to them. Discard any with broken shells or any that refuse to close when tapped. Put the mussels into a large pan with just the water on their shells and cook, covered, over a high heat for 3–4 minutes, shaking the pan occasionally, until all the mussels have opened. Discard any mussels that remain closed. Drain, reserving the cooking liquid, and set aside until cool enough to handle.

2 Strain the cooking liquid into a clean pan and simmer until reduced to about 1 tablespoon. Put the liquid into a food processor with the basil, garlic, pine kernels (nuts) and Parmesan and process until finely chopped. Add the olive oil and breadcrumbs and process until well mixed.

3 Open the mussels and loosen from their shells, discarding the empty half of the shell. Divide the pesto breadcrumbs between the mussels.

4 Cook under a preheated grill (broiler) until the breadcrumbs are crisp, golden and the mussels heated through. Serve immediately with slices of tomato and garnish with basil leaves.

VARIATION

If you want an alternative to pine kernels (nuts) add 80 g/3 oz roughly chopped, drained sun-dried tomatoes in oil to the pesto instead.

Curried Mussel Tartlets

Mussels absorb other flavours well and are therefore very versatile. Here they are cooked in a creamy curried tart filling with a crisp, nutty pastry shell.

Serves 6

INGREDIENTS

175 g/6 oz/1½ cups plain (all-purpose) flour
½ tsp turmeric
½ tsp salt
80 g/3 oz/6 tbsp butter, cut into small pieces
25 g/1 oz finely chopped walnuts
salad, to serve

CURRIED MUSSEL FILLING:
450 g/1 lb live mussels
2 tsp vegetable oil
2 garlic cloves, finely chopped
1 tsp grated ginger root
1 tsp mild curry paste
200 ml/7 fl oz/¾ cup double (heavy) cream
2 egg yolks
2 tbsp chopped fresh coriander
salt and pepper

1 To make the pastry, sift the flour, turmeric and salt into the bowl of a food processor or large bowl. Add the butter and process, or rub in with your fingers, until the mixture resembles fine breadcrumbs. Stir in the walnuts and add 2 tablespoons cold water. Process or mix briefly until the dough starts to come together, adding a little more water if necessary. Do not overprocess. Turn the dough on to a lightly floured surface and knead briefly until smooth. Wrap in cling film (plastic wrap) and leave to rest in the refrigerator for 30 minutes.

2 Clean the mussels by scrubbing or scraping the shells and pulling out any beards that are attached to them. Discard any with broken shells or any that refuse to close when tapped. Put the mussels into a large pan with just the water on their shells and cook, covered, over a high heat for 3–4 minutes, shaking the pan occasionally, until all the mussels have opened. Discard any mussels that remain closed, drain and set aside until cool enough to handle. Remove the mussels from their shells.

3 Heat the oil in a small frying pan (skillet), add the garlic and ginger. Stir-fry for 1 minute before stirring in the curry paste and mixing well. Remove from the heat and add the cream. Set aside and allow to cool.

4 Divide the pastry into 6 equal pieces. Roll out each piece thinly and use to line 6 x 9 cm/3½ inch individual tartlet tins. Carefully line the pastry with foil and fill with baking beans. Place in a preheated oven, at 200°C/400°F/Gas Mark 6, for 10 minutes. Remove the foil and beans and cook for a further 5 minutes. Remove from the oven and allow to cool slightly. Reduce oven temperature to 180°C/350°F/Gas Mark 4.

5 Divide the cooked mussels between the cooled pastry cases. Whisk the egg yolks and coriander into the cooled cream mixture. Then season and pour the mixture into the pastry cases to cover the mussels. Bake in the preheated oven for 25 minutes until the filling has just set and the pastry is golden. Allow to cool and serve warm with salad.

Calamari

The batter may not be traditional, but this is a perfect dish to serve as part of a selection of tapas, or little dishes, with drinks as they do in Spain.

Serves 4

INGREDIENTS

115 g/4 oz/1 cup plain (all purpose) flour
1 tsp salt
2 eggs
175 ml/6 fl oz/¾ cup soda water
450 g/1 lb prepared squid (see method), cut into rings
vegetable oil, for deep-frying
lemon wedges, to serve
parsley sprigs, to garnish

1 Sift the flour into a bowl with the salt. Add the eggs and half the soda water and whisk together until smooth. Gradually whisk in the remaining soda water until the batter is smooth. Set aside.

2 To prepare whole squid, hold the body firmly and grasp the tentacles just inside the body. Pull firmly to remove the innards. Find the transparent 'backbone' and remove. Grasp the wings on the outside of the body and pull to remove the outer skin. Trim the tentacles just below the beak and reserve.

3 Wash the body and tentacles under running water. Slice the body across into 1 cm/½ inch rings. Drain well on paper towels.

4 Meanwhile, fill a deep saucepan about a third full with vegetable oil and heat to 190°F/ 375°F or until a cube of bread browns in 30 seconds.

5 Dip the squid rings and tentacles into the batter, a few at a time, and drop into the hot oil. Fry for 1–2 minutes until crisp and golden. Drain on paper towels. Cook all the squid this way. Serve immediately while still hot with garnished with lemon wedges and parsley.

COOK'S TIP

If you don't like the idea of cleaning squid yourself, get your fishmonger to do it. Sometimes, squid is even sold already cut into rings. Alternatively, you could use prepared baby squid for this dish.

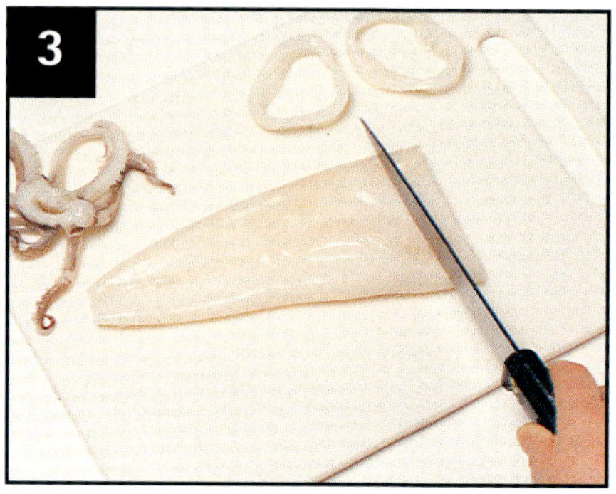

Stuffed Squid

This is a very typical Greek recipe for stuffing squid. Most large supermarkets with fish counters sell baby squid already cleaned.

Serves 4

INGREDIENTS

12 baby squid, cleaned
1 tsp salt
4 tbsp olive oil
1 small onion, finely chopped
1 garlic clove, finely chopped
40g /1½ oz basmati rice
1 tbsp seedless raisins
1 tbsp pine kernels (nuts), toasted
1 tbsp chopped fresh flat-leaf parsley
400 g/14 oz can chopped tomatoes
25 g/1 oz sun-dried tomatoes in oil, drained and finely chopped
120 ml/4 fl oz/½ cup dry white wine
salt and pepper
crusty bread, to serve

1 Separate the tentacles from the body of the squid. Chop the tentacles and set aside. Rub the squid tubes inside and out with the salt and set aside while you prepare the stuffing.

2 Heat 1 tablespoon of the olive oil in a frying pan (skillet) and add the onion and garlic. Cook for 4–5 minutes until softened and lightly browned. Add the chopped tentacles and fry for 2–3 minutes. Add the rice, raisins, pine kernels (nuts) and parsley and seasoning. Remove from the heat.

3 Allow the rice mixture to cool slightly and spoon it into the squid tubes, about three quarters full to allow the rice to expand. You may need to open the squid tubes a little by making a small cut. Secure each filled squid with a cocktail stick.

4 Heat the remaining oil in a large flameproof casserole. Add the squid and fry for a few minutes on all sides until lightly browned. Add the tomatoes, sun-dried tomatoes, wine and seasoning. Bake in a preheated oven at 180°C/350°F/Gas Mark 4, for 45 minutes. Serve hot or cold with plenty of crusty bread.

COOK'S TIP

If you have difficulty finding baby squid, larger ones work very well and the cooking time is the same. Use cleaned squid weighing 225 g/8 oz in total for the amount of stuffing in this recipe.

Tempura Whitebait

Tempura is a classic Japanese batter made with egg, flour and water. The batter is very cold and very lumpy, which gives the finished dish its characteristic appearance. It should be eaten straight away.

Serves 4

INGREDIENTS

450 g/1 lb whitebait (smelts), thawed if frozen
100 g/3½ oz/¾ cup plain flour
50 g/1¾ oz/⅓ cup cornflour
½ tsp salt
200 ml/7 fl oz /1 cup cold water
1 egg
a few ice cubes
vegetable oil, for deep-frying

CHILLI AND LIME MAYONNAISE:
1 egg yolk
1 tbsp lime juice
1 fresh red chilli, deseeded and finely chopped
2 tbsp chopped fresh coriander
200 ml/7 fl oz/1 cup light olive oil
salt and pepper

1 To make the mayonnaise, in the bowl of a food processor or blender, mix together the egg yolk, lime juice, chilli, coriander and seasoning until foaming. With the machine running, gradually add the olive oil, drop by drop to begin with, until the mixture begins to thicken. Continue adding the oil in a steady stream. Adjust seasoning and add a little hot water if the mixture seems too thick. Put to one side.

2 For the tempura whitebait, wash and dry the fish. Set aside on paper towels. In a large bowl, sift together the plain flour, cornflour and salt. Whisk together the water, egg and ice cubes and pour on to the flour. Whisk briefly until the mixture is runny, but still lumpy with dry bits of flour still apparent.

3 Meanwhile, fill a deep saucepan about a third full with vegetable oil and heat to 190°F/ 375°F or until a cube of bread browns in 30 seconds.

4 Dip the whitebait, a few at a time, into the batter and carefully drop into the hot oil. Fry for 1 minute until the batter is crisp but not browned. Drain on paper towels. Cook all the whitebait this way. Serve hot with the chilli and lime mayonnaise.

1

2

4

Smoked Mackerel Pâté

This is a quick and easy pâté with plenty of flavour. It originates from Goa, on the west coast of India, an area famous for its seafood.

Serves 4

INGREDIENTS

200g /7 oz smoked mackerel fillet
1 small, hot green chilli, deseeded and chopped
1 garlic clove, chopped
3 tbsp fresh coriander leaves
150 ml/5 fl oz pint/⅔ cup soured cream
1 small red onion, chopped
2 tbsp lime juice
salt and pepper
4 slices white bread, crusts removed

1 Skin and flake the mackerel fillet, removing any small bones. Put the flesh in the bowl of a food processor along with the chilli, garlic, coriander and soured cream. Blend until smooth.

2 Transfer the mixture to a bowl and mix in the onion and lime juice. Season to taste. The pâté will seem very soft at this stage but will firm up in the refrigerator. Refrigerate for several hours or overnight if possible.

3 To make the melba toasts, place the trimmed bread slices under a preheated medium grill (broiler) and toast lightly on both sides. Split the toasts in half horizontally, then cut each across diagonally to form 4 triangles per slice.

4 Put the triangles, untoasted side up, under the grill (broiler) and toast until golden and curled at the edges. Serve warm or cold with the smoked mackerel pâté.

COOK'S TIP

This pâté is also very good served with crudities.

Smoked Haddock Salad

Smoked haddock has an affinity with eggs.
Here it is teamed with hard-boiled quail's eggs and topped with a creamy chive dressing.

Serves 4

INGREDIENTS

350 g/12 oz smoked haddock fillet
4 tbsp olive oil
1 tbsp lemon juice
2 tbsp soured cream
1 tbsp hot water
2 tbsp chopped fresh chives
1 plum tomato, peeled, deseeded and diced
8 quail's eggs
4 thick slices granary or multigrain bread
115 g/4 oz mixed salad leaves
chives, to garnish
salt and pepper

1 Fill a large frying pan (skillet) with water and bring to the boil. Add the smoked haddock fillet, cover and remove from the heat. Leave for 10 minutes until the fish is tender. Lift from the poaching water, drain and leave until cool enough to handle. Flake the flesh, removing any small bones. Set aside. Discard the poaching water.

2 Whisk together the olive oil, lemon juice, soured cream, hot water, chives and seasoning. Stir in the tomato. Set aside.

3 Bring a small saucepan of water to the boil. Carefully lower the quail's eggs into the water. Cook the eggs for 3–4 minutes from when the water returns to the boil (3 minutes for a slightly soft centre, 4 minutes for a firm centre). Drain immediately and refresh under cold running water. Carefully peel the eggs, cut in half lengthways and set aside.

4 Toast the granary bread and cut each across diagonally to form 4 triangles. Arrange 2 halves on 4 serving plates. Top with the salad leaves, then the flaked fish and finally the quail's eggs. Spoon over the dressing and garnish with a few extra chives.

COOK'S TIP

When buying smoked haddock, and smoked fish in general, look for undyed fish, which is always superior in quality.

Thai Fish Cakes with Sweet & Sour Chilli Dipping Sauce

If you can find them, use small chillies, called bird's eye, for the dipping sauce. They are very hot however, so remove the seeds if you prefer.

Serves 4

INGREDIENTS

- 450 g/1 lb firm white fish, such as hake, haddock or cod, skinned and roughly chopped
- 1 tbsp Thai fish sauce
- 1 tbsp red curry paste (see Red Prawn Curry, page 102)
- 1 kaffir lime leaf, finely shredded
- 2 tbsp chopped fresh coriander
- 1 egg
- 1 tsp brown sugar
- large pinch salt
- 40 g/1½ oz green beans, thinly sliced crossways
- vegetable oil, for shallow-frying

SWEET AND SOUR DIPPING SAUCE:

- 4 tbsp sugar
- 1 tbsp cold water
- 3 tbsp white rice vinegar
- 2 small, hot chillies, finely chopped
- 1 tbsp fish sauce

1 For the fish cakes, put the fish, fish sauce, curry paste, lime leaf, coriander, egg, sugar and salt into the bowl of a food processor. Process until smooth. Scrape into a bowl and stir in the green beans. Set aside.

2 To make the dipping sauce, put the sugar, water and rice vinegar into a small saucepan and heat gently until the sugar has dissolved. Bring to the boil and simmer for 2 minutes. Remove from the heat and stir in the chillies and fish sauce and leave to cool.

3 Heat a frying pan (skillet) with enough oil to generously cover the bottom. Divide the fish mixture into 16 little balls. Flatten the balls into little patties and fry in the hot oil for 1–2 minutes each side until golden. Drain on paper towels. Serve hot with the dipping sauce.

COOK'S TIP

It isn't necessary to use the most expensive cut of white fish in this recipe as the other flavours are very strong. Use whatever is cheapest.

Maryland Crab Cakes with Basil & Tomato Dressing

These crab cakes contain a high proportion of crabmeat and are therefore very light. You can serve them with a warm basil and tomato dressing but they are also delicious with good-quality mayonnaise.

Serves 4

INGREDIENTS

225 g/8 oz potatoes, cut into chunks
450 g/1 lb/2 cups cooked white and brown crab meat, thawed if frozen
6 spring onions, finely chopped
1 small red chilli, deseeded and finely chopped
3 tbsp mayonnaise
2 tbsp plain (all purpose) flour
1 egg, lightly beaten
115 g/4 oz/1 cup fresh white breadcrumbs
vegetable oil, for shallow frying
salt and pepper
lemon slices and dill, to serve

DRESSING:
5 tbsp olive oil
1 tbsp lemon juice
1 large ripe tomato, peeled, deseeded and diced
3 tbsp chopped fresh basil
salt and pepper

1 Cook the potatoes in boiling salted water for 15–20 minutes until tender. Drain well and mash.

2 In a large bowl, mix together the crab meat, spring onions, chilli and mayonnaise. Add the mashed potato, seasoning and mix together well. Shape the mixture into 8 cakes.

3 Put the flour, egg and breadcrumbs into separate bowls. Dip the cakes first into the flour, then the egg and finally the breadcrumbs to coat. Refrigerate for 30 minutes.

4 In a large frying pan (skillet), heat enough vegetable oil to generously cover the bottom of the pan. Add the cakes, in batches if necessary, and cook for 3–4 minutes on each side until golden and crisp. Drain on paper towels and keep warm while you cook the remaining cakes.

5 Meanwhile, for the dressing, put the oil, lemon juice and tomato in a small saucepan and heat gently for 2–3 minutes. Remove from the heat and stir in the basil and seasoning.

6 Divide the fish cakes between 4 serving plates. Spoon over the dressing. Serve immediately.

Lime & Basil Cured Salmon

It is very important to use fresh salmon for this dish. The salt and sugar draw the moisture from the fish, leaving it raw but cured and full of flavour.

Serves 6

INGREDIENTS

900 g/2 lb very fresh salmon fillet, from the head end, skinned
50 g/1¾ oz sugar
50 g/1¾ oz sea salt
5 tbsp chopped fresh basil
finely grated rind of 2 limes
1 tsp white peppercorns, lightly crushed

DRESSING:
200 ml/7 fl oz/¾ cup rice vinegar
5 tbsp sugar
finely grated rind of 1 lime
½ tsp English mustard
3 tbsp chopped fresh basil
1 tbsp Japanese pickled ginger, finely shredded

150 g/5½ oz mixed salad leaves, to serve

TO GARNISH:
lime wedges
basil leaves

1 Remove any small pin bones that remain in the salmon fillet. Wash and dry the fish. Place the salmon in a large non-metallic dish and sprinkle evenly with the sugar, sea salt, basil, lime rind and peppercorns. Cover and chill for 24–48 hours, turning the fish occasionally.

2 For the dressing, put the rice vinegar and sugar in a small saucepan and stir gently over a low heat until the sugar has dissolved. Then, bring to the boil and simmer for 5–6 minutes until the liquid is reduced by about one third. Remove the saucepan from the heat and stir in the lime rind and mustard. Put the saucepan to one side.

3 Remove the salmon fillet from the marinade, wiping off any excess with paper towels. Slice very thinly.

4 To serve, stir the chopped basil and ginger into the dressing. Toss the salad leaves with a little of the dressing and arrange on 6 serving plates. Divide the salmon slices between the plates and drizzle a little dressing over. Garnish with lime wedges and basil leaves.

Hot-smoked Salmon Scramble

Hot-smoked salmon is increasingly available and is such a treat. Unlike traditional smoked salmon, the fish is smoked in a hot environment so that the flesh cooks conventionally but has a wonderful smoky flavour. This fish is particularly juicy and tender.

Serves 4

INGREDIENTS

50 g/1¾ oz/¼ cup butter
8 eggs, lightly beaten
4 tbsp double (heavy) cream
225 g/8 oz skinless, boneless hot-smoked salmon, flaked
2 tbsp chopped fresh mixed herbs such as chives, basil, parsley
4 English muffins, split
extra butter, for spreading
salt and pepper
chopped fresh chives, to garnish
lemon wedges, to serve

1 Melt the butter in a large frying pan (skillet) and when it begins to foam, add the eggs. Leave for a moment to start to set and slowly stir and move the set eggs away from the bottom of the pan to allow uncooked egg to take its place. Leave again for a moment and repeat.

2 Before all the egg has set, stir in the double (heavy) cream, flaked salmon and chopped herbs. Stir to incorporate. Do not overcook the eggs.

3 Meanwhile, toast the split muffins on both sides. Spread with more butter if liked. Place 2 muffin halves on each of 4 plates.

4 When the eggs are cooked, divide between the muffins. Sprinkle over a few chopped chives, season and serve while still warm with a lemon wedge.

VARIATION

If you have difficulty finding hot-smoked salmon, you could substitute conventional smoked salmon, chopped.

Griddled Smoked Salmon

It is best to buy packets of smoked salmon strips for this recipe as they lend themselves to folding more easily than freshly sliced salmon.

Serves 4

INGREDIENTS

- 350 g/12 oz sliced smoked salmon
- 1 tsp Dijon mustard
- 1 garlic clove, crushed
- 2 tsp chopped fresh dill
- 2 tsp sherry vinegar
- 4 tbsp olive oil
- 114 g/4 oz mixed salad leaves
- salt and pepper

1 Take the slices of smoked salmon and fold them, making two folds accordion style, so that they form little parcels.

2 Whisk the mustard, garlic, dill, vinegar and seasoning together. Gradually whisk in the olive oil to form a light emulsion.

3 Heat a ridged griddle pan until smoking. Cook the salmon parcels on one side only for 2–3 minutes until heated through and marked from the pan.

4 Meanwhile, dress the salad leaves with some of the vinaigrette and divide between 4 serving plates. Top with the cooked smoked salmon, cooked side up. Drizzle with the remaining dressing.

COOK'S TIP

Smoked salmon is very expensive. This recipe would also work well with smoked trout.

1

2

3

Salmon Tartare

It is very important to use the freshest possible fish for this dish. The fish is not cooked, but cured with lemon and lime juice so that it has the appearance and texture of having been cooked.

Serves 6

INGREDIENTS

900 g/2 lb very fresh salmon fillet, skinned
3 tbsp lemon juice
3 tbsp lime juice
2 tsp sugar
1 tsp Dijon mustard
1 tbsp chopped fresh dill
1 tbsp chopped fresh basil
2 tbsp olive oil
50 g/1¾ oz rocket (arugula)
handful basil leaves
50 g/1¾ oz mixed salad leaves
salt and pepper

TO GARNISH:
dill sprigs
basil leaves

1 Cut the salmon into very tiny dice and season. Put into a large bowl.

2 Mix together the lemon juice, lime juice, sugar, mustard, dill, basil and olive oil. Pour over the salmon and mix well. Set aside for 15–20 minutes until the fish becomes opaque.

3 Meanwhile, mix together the rocket (arugula), basil leaves and salad leaves. Divide between serving plates.

4 To serve the salmon, fill a small ramekin or mini pudding basin with the mixture and turn out on to the centre of the salad leaves. Garnish with dill sprigs and basil leaves.

VARIATION

Haddock also responds very well to this treatment. Use half the quantity of salmon and an equal weight of haddock.

1

2

4

Gravadlax

You need two pieces of salmon fillet for this dish, approximately the same size. Ask your fishmonger to remove all the bones and scale the fish for you.

Serves 6

INGREDIENTS

2 x 450 g/1 lb salmon fillets, with skin on
6 tbsp roughly chopped fresh dill
115 g/4 oz sea salt50 g/1¾ oz sugar
1 tbsp white peppercorns, roughly crushed
12 slices brown bread, buttered, to serve

GARNISH
lemon slices
dill sprigs

1 Wash the salmon fillets and dry with paper towels. Put one fillet, skin side down, in a non-metallic dish.

2 Mix together the dill, sea salt, sugar and peppercorns. Spread this mixture over the first fillet of fish and place the second fillet, skin side up, on top. Put a plate, the same size as the fish, on top and put a weight on the plate (3 or 4 cans of tomatoes or similar will do).

3 Refrigerate for 2 days, turning the fish about every 12 hours and basting with any juices which have come out of the fish.

4 Remove the salmon from the brine and slice thinly, without slicing the skin, as you would smoked salmon. Cut the brown bread into triangles and serve with the salmon. Garnish with lemon wedges and sprigs of fresh dill.

COOK'S TIP

You can brush the marinade off the salmon before slicing, but the line of green along the edge of the salmon is quite attractive and, of course, full of flavour.

2

3

4

Thai Crab Omelette

Don't be put off by the long list of ingredients.
The omelette is served cold and so can be made entirely ahead of time.

Serves 4

INGREDIENTS

- 225 g/8 oz white crab meat, fresh or thawed if frozen
- 3 spring onions (scallions), finely chopped
- 1 tbsp chopped fresh coriander
- 1 tbsp chopped fresh chives
- pinch cayenne pepper
- 1 tbsp vegetable oil
- 2 garlic cloves, crushed
- 1 tsp freshly grated ginger root
- 1 red chilli, deseeded and finely chopped
- 2 tbsp lime juice
- 2 lime leaves, shredded
- 2 tsp sugar
- 2 tsp Thai fish sauce
- 3 eggs
- 4 tbsp coconut cream
- 1 tsp salt
- 1 tbsp vegetable oil
- spring onion, slithers, to garnish

1 Put the crab meat into a bowl and check for any small pieces of shell. Add the spring onions (scallions), coriander, chives and cayenne and set aside.

2 Heat the vegetable oil and add the garlic, ginger and chilli and stir-fry for 30 seconds. Add the lime juice, lime leaves, sugar and fish sauce. Simmer for 3–4 minutes until reduced. Remove from the heat and allow to cool. Add to the crab mixture and set aside.

3 Lightly beat the eggs with the coconut cream and salt. In a frying pan (skillet), heat the vegetable oil over a medium heat. Add the egg mixture and as it sets on the bottom, carefully pull the edges in toward the centre, allowing unset egg to run underneath.

4 When the egg is nearly set, spoon the crab mixture down the centre. Cook a further 1–2 minutes to finish cooking the egg, then turn the omelette out of the pan on to a serving dish. Allow to cool then refrigerate for 2–3 hours or overnight. Cut into 4 pieces and garnish with spring onion.

COOK'S TIP

You can also serve this omelette warm. After adding the crab, cook for 3–4 minutes to allow the mixture to heat through then serve immediately.

Soups & Stews

Using seafood in soups and stews makes wonderful sense. It doesn't require much cooking, making it ideal as a basis for a mid-week supper, and it combines well with an enormous variety of flavours.

It seems that only in the English-speaking world fish is undervalued. Other parts of the world use fish as a staple part of their diet and this chapter includes many dishes from a variety of places.

Don't worry though, most of the more unusual ingredients are readily available nowadays from larger supermarkets or from specialist shops. Soups like Thai Fish Soup, Malaysian Seafood Laksa and Chinese Crab & Sweetcorn Soup illustrate the diversity of the recipes. Some of the soups are very subtly flavoured and ideal as a first course at a dinner party, such as the Creamy Scallop Soup.

Others are much more substantial and could easily be served as a main course, like the Cullen Skink. There are lots of stews and curries to choose from as well, from Red Prawn Curry to Goan Fish Curry and from Cotriade to Spanish Fish Stew.

Thai Fish Soup

This is also known as Tom Yam Gung. Oriental supermarkets may sell tom yam sauce ready prepared in jars, sometimes labelled 'Chillies in Oil'. This is a perfectly acceptable substitute and will certainly save on time.

Serves 4

INGREDIENTS

- 450 ml/16 fl oz/2 cups light chicken stock
- 2 lime leaves, chopped
- 5 cm/2 inch piece lemon grass, chopped
- 3 tbsp lemon juice
- 3 tbsp Thai fish sauce
- 2 small, hot green chillies, deseeded and finely chopped
- ½ tsp sugar
- 8 small shiitake mushrooms or 8 straw mushrooms, halved
- 450 g/1 lb raw prawns (shrimp), peeled if necessary and de-veined
- spring onions (scallions), to garnish

TOM YAM SAUCE:

- 4 tbsp vegetable oil
- 5 garlic cloves, finely chopped
- 1 large shallot, finely chopped
- 2 large hot dried red chillies, roughly chopped
- 1 tbsp dried shrimp (optional)
- 1 tbsp Thai fish sauce
- 2 tsp sugar

1 First make the tom yam sauce. Heat the oil in a small frying pan (skillet) and add the garlic. Cook for a few seconds until the garlic just browns. Remove with a slotted spoon and set aside. Add the shallot to the same oil and fry until browned and crisp. Remove with a slotted spoon and set aside. Add the chillies and fry until they darken. Remove from the oil and drain on paper towels. Remove the pan from the hob, reserve oil.

2 In a small food processor or spice grinder, grind the dried shrimp, if using, then add the reserved chillies, garlic and shallots. Grind together to a smooth paste. Return the pan with the original oil to a low heat, add the paste and warm. Add the fish sauce and sugar and mix. Remove from the heat.

3 In a large saucepan, heat together the stock and 2 tablespoons of the tom yam sauce. Add the lime leaves, lemon grass, lemon juice, fish sauce, chillies and sugar. Simmer for 2 minutes.

4 Add the mushrooms and prawns (shrimp) and cook a further 2–3 minutes until the prawns (shrimp) are cooked. Ladle in to warm bowls and serve immediately, garnished with spring onion (scallions).

Cullen Skink

This is a traditional, creamy Scottish soup of smoked haddock and potato. As the smoked haddock has quite a strong flavour, I have mixed it with some fresh cod.

Serves 4

INGREDIENTS

- 225 g/8 oz undyed smoked haddock fillet
- 25 g/1 oz/2 tbsp butter
- 1 onion, finely chopped
- 600 ml/1 pint/2½ cups milk
- 350 g/12 oz potatoes, cut into dice
- 350 g/12 oz cod, boned, skinned and cubed
- 150 ml/¼ pint/⅔ cup double (heavy) cream
- 2 tbsp chopped fresh parsley
- lemon juice, to taste
- salt and pepper

TO GARNISH:

- lemon slices
- parsley sprigs

1 Put the haddock fillet in a large frying pan (skillet) and cover with boiling water. Leave for 10 minutes. Drain, reserving 300 ml/½ pint of the soaking water. Flake the fish, taking care to remove all the bones.

2 Heat the butter in a large saucepan and add the onion. Cook gently for 10 minutes until softened. Add the milk and bring to a gentle simmer before adding the potato. Cook for 10 minutes.

3 Add the reserved haddock flakes and cod. Simmer a further 10 minutes until the cod is tender.

4 Remove about one third of the fish and potatoes, put in a food processor and blend until smooth. Alternatively, push through a sieve into a bowl. Return to the soup with the cream, parsley and seasoning. Taste and add a little lemon juice, if liked. Add a little of the reserved soaking water if the soup seems too thick. Reheat gently and serve immediately.

COOK'S TIP

Look for Finnan haddock, if you can find it. Do not use yellow dyed haddock fillet, which is often actually whiting and not haddock at all.

New England Clam Chowder

A chowder is a thick soup whose main ingredients are milk and potatoes, to which other flavours are added. This is a classic version from New England, flavoured with fresh clams.

Serves 4

INGREDIENTS

900 g/2 lb live clams
4 rashers rindless streaky bacon, chopped
25 g/1 oz/2 tbsp butter
1 onion, chopped
1 tbsp chopped fresh thyme
1 large potato, diced
1 bay leaf
300 ml/½ pint/1¼ cups milk
150 ml/5 fl oz/$1^2/_3$ cup double (heavy) cream
1 tbsp chopped fresh parsley
salt and pepper
reserve 8 clams in their shells, to garnish (see Cook's Tip)

1 Scrub the clams and put into a large saucepan with a splash of water. Cook over a high heat for 3–4 minutes until all the clams have opened. Discard any that remain closed. Strain the clams, reserving the cooking liquid. Set aside until cool enough to handle.

2 Remove the clams from their shells, roughly chop if large, and set aside.

3 In a clean saucepan, fry the bacon until browned and crisp. Drain on paper towels. Add the butter to the same pan and when it has melted, add the onion. Cook for 4–5 minutes until softened but not coloured. Add the thyme and cook briefly before adding the diced potato, reserved clam cooking liquid, milk and bay leaf. Bring to the boil and simmer for 10 minutes until the potato is tender but not falling apart.

4 Transfer to a food processor and blend until smooth or push through a sieve into a bowl.

5 Add the reserved clams, bacon and the cream. Simmer a further 2–3 minutes until heated through. Season to taste. Stir in the chopped parsley and serve.

COOK'S TIP

For a smart presentation, reserve 8 clams in their shells. Sit 2 on top of each bowl of soup to serve.

5

3

5

Malaysian Seafood Laksa

As with many Oriental dishes, the list of ingredients is dauntingly long but don't be put off.

Serves 4

INGREDIENTS

8 raw tiger prawns (jumbo shrimp)
1 small squid, about 115 g/4 oz cleaned weight
4 tbsp vegetable oil
900 ml/1½ pints/3¾ cups light chicken stock
225 g/8 oz medium egg noodles
115 g/4 oz bean-sprouts
400 ml/14 oz can coconut milk
2 tsp muscovado sugar
1 tsp salt

LAKSA SPICE PASTE:
3 large dried red chillies
25 g/1 oz dried shrimp (optional)
2 stalks lemon grass, chopped
25 g/1 oz macadamia nuts
2 garlic cloves, chopped
2 tsp chopped fresh ginger root
1 tsp turmeric
1 small onion, chopped
1 tsp ground coriander
3 tbsp water

TO GARNISH:
55 g/1¾ oz cucumber, cut into matchsticks
1 tbsp chopped fresh coriander
1 tbsp chopped fresh mint
4 spring onions, thinly sliced
1 red chilli, sliced into rings
1 lime, quartered

1 For the laksa spice paste, put the dried chillies into a bowl and pour over enough boiling water to cover. Leave to soak for 10 minutes until softened. Drain and remove the seeds if you prefer. Put into a food processor with the remaining spice paste ingredients. Blend until smooth and then set aside.

2 Peel the prawns if necessary and de-vein. Split the squid down one side and open out flat. Lightly score the underside of the flesh using a sharp knife, first one way then the other. This helps to tenderise the flesh. Cut into 2.5 cm/1 inch squares and set aside.

3 Heat the vegetable oil in a large saucepan and fry the spice paste gently for 5–6 minutes until it smells very fragrant. Add the stock, bring to the boil, cover and simmer gently for 20 minutes.

4 Cook the egg noodles according to the packet instructions, drain well and set aside. Blanch the bean-sprouts for 1 minute and refresh under cold water. Drain well and set aside with the noodles.

5 Add the coconut milk to the stock and simmer for 3 minutes. Add the prawns, squid, sugar and salt and simmer for just 4 minutes until the seafood is tender.

6 Divide the noodles and bean-sprouts between 4 warmed soup bowls. Spoon the hot soup over this mixture and garnish each bowl with cucumber, coriander, mint, spring onions, red chilli and lime wedges serving any extra in small bowls.

Chinese Crab & Sweetcorn Soup

This soup is based on the classic Chinese chicken and sweetcorn soup, but the delicate flavour of the crab works very well.

Serves 4

INGREDIENTS

1 tbsp vegetable oil
1 small onion, finely chopped
1 garlic clove, finely chopped
1 tsp grated fresh ginger root
1 small red chilli, deseeded and finely chopped
2 tbsp dry sherry or Chinese rice wine
225 g/8 oz fresh white crab meat
326 g/11 oz can sweetcorn, drained
600 ml/1 pint/2½ light chicken stock
1 tbsp light soy sauce
2 tbsp chopped fresh coriander
2 eggs, beaten
salt and pepper

1 Heat the oil in a large saucepan and add the onion. Cook gently for 5 minutes until softened. Add the garlic, ginger and chilli and cook for a further minute.

2 Add the sherry or rice wine and bubble until reduced by half. Add the crab meat, sweetcorn, chicken stock and soy sauce. Bring to the boil and simmer gently for 5 minutes. Stir in the coriander. Season to taste.

3 Remove from the heat and pour in the eggs. Wait for a few seconds and then stir well, to break the eggs into ribbons. Serve immediately, garnished with chilli flowers.

COOK'S TIP

For convenience, you could use canned crab meat. Make sure it is well drained before adding it to the soup.

Creamy Scallop Soup

This is a very delicately flavoured soup which, like all seafood, should not be overcooked. A sprinkling of parsley just before serving makes a pretty contrast to the creamy colour of the soup.

Serves 4

INGREDIENTS

50 g/1¾ oz/¼ cup butter
1 onion, finely chopped
450 g/1 lb potatoes, diced
600 ml/1 pint/2½ cups hot fish stock
350 g/12 oz prepared scallops, including corals if available
300 ml/½ pint/1¼ cups milk
2 egg yolks
90 ml/3 fl oz/¾ cup double (heavy) cream
salt and pepper
1 tbsp chopped fresh parsley, to garnish

1 Melt the butter in a large saucepan over a gentle heat. Add the onions and cook very gently for 10 minutes until the onions are softened but not coloured. Add the potatoes and seasoning, cover and cook for a further 10 minutes over a very low heat.

2 Pour on the hot fish stock, bring to the boil and simmer for a further 10–15 minutes until the potatoes are tender.

3 Meanwhile, prepare the scallops. If the corals are available, roughly chop and set aside. Roughly chop the white meat and put in a second saucepan with the milk. Bring to a gentle simmer and cook for 6–8 minutes until the scallops are just tender.

4 When the potatoes are cooked, transfer them and their cooking liquid to a food processor or blender and blend to a purée. Alternatively, press through a nylon sieve. Return the mixture to a clean saucepan with the scallops and their milk and the pieces of coral, if using.

5 Whisk together the egg yolks and cream and add to the soup, off the heat. Return the soup to a very gentle heat and, stirring constantly, reheat the soup until it thickens slightly. Do not boil or the soup will curdle. Adjust seasoning and serve immediately, sprinkled with fresh parsley.

COOK'S TIP

The soup can be made in advance up to the point where the cream and eggs are added. This should only be done just before serving.

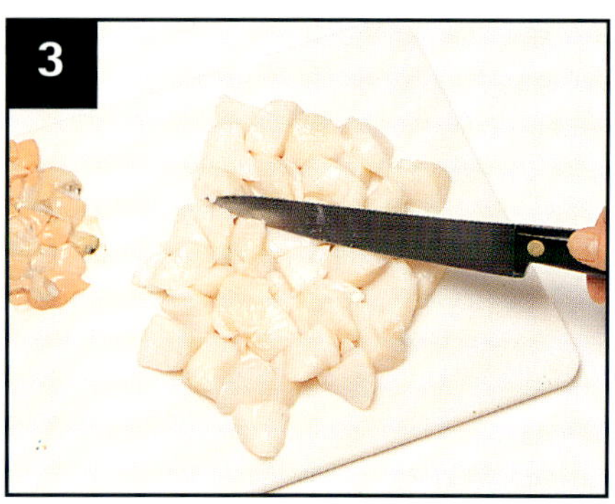
3

4

5

Curried Mussel Soup

Surprisingly, this soup is French in origin. This version, however, uses freshly roasted spices rather than the bland curry powder popular in France.

Serves 4

INGREDIENTS

- 1/2 tsp coriander seeds
- 1/2 tsp cumin seeds
- 900 g/2 lb live mussels
- 100 ml/3 1/2 fl oz/scant 1/2 cup white wine
- 50 g/1 3/4 oz/1/4 cup butter
- 1 onion, finely chopped
- 1 garlic clove, finely chopped
- 1 tsp freshly grated ginger root
- 1 tsp turmeric
- pinch cayenne pepper
- 600 ml/1 pint/2 1/2 cups fish stock
- 4 tbsp double (heavy) cream
- 25 g/1 oz/2 tbsp butter, softened
- 25 g/1 oz/2 tbsp flour
- 2 tbsp chopped fresh coriander, to garnish
- salt and pepper

1 Fry the coriander and cumin seeds in a dry frying pan (skillet) until they begin to smell aromatic and start to pop. Grind to a powder with a pestle a mortar. Set aside.

2 Clean the mussels by scrubbing or scraping the shells and pulling out any beards that are attached to them. Discard any with broken shells or any that do not close when tapped. Put the mussels into a large pan with the wine and cook, covered, over a high heat for 3–4 minutes, shaking the pan occasionally, until all the mussels have opened. Discard any mussels that remain closed. Drain, reserving the cooking liquid, and set aside until the mussels are cool enough to handle. Remove about two thirds of the mussels from their shells and set them all aside. Strain the mussel cooking liquid through a fine sieve.

3 Heat half the butter in a large saucepan and add the onion. Fry gently for 4–5 minutes until softened, but not coloured. Add the garlic and ginger and cook for a further minute before adding the roasted and ground spices, the turmeric and cayenne. Fry for 1 minute before adding the fish stock, reserved mussel cooking liquid and cream. Simmer for 10 minutes.

4 Cream together the butter and flour to a thick paste. Add the paste to the simmering soup and stir until dissolved and the soup has thickened slightly. Add the mussels and warm for 2 minutes. Garnish with parsley and serve.

Clam & Sorrel Soup

This recipe is intended to be served in small quantities. It is very rich and full of flavour.

Serves 4

INGREDIENTS

900 g/2 lb live clams, scrubbed
1 onion, finely chopped
150 ml/5 fl oz/2/3 cup dry white wine
50 g/1 3/4 oz/1/4 cup butter
1 small carrot, finely diced
2 shallots, finely diced
1 stick celery, finely diced
2 bay leaves
150 ml/5 fl oz/2/3 cup double (heavy) cream
25 g/1 oz/1 cup loosely packed shredded sorrel
pepper
crusty bread, to serve
dill, to garnish

1 Put the clams into a large saucepan with the onion and wine. Cover and cook over a high heat for 3–4 minutes until the clams have opened. Strain, reserving the cooking liquid, but discarding the onion. Set aside the clams until they are cool enough to handle.

2 In a clean saucepan, melt the butter over a low heat. Add the carrot, shallots and celery and cook very gently for 10 minutes until softened but not coloured. Add the reserved cooking liquid and bay leaves and simmer for a further 10 minutes.

3 Meanwhile, roughly chop the clams, if large. Add to the soup with the cream and sorrel. Simmer a further 2–3 minutes until the sorrel has collapsed. Season with pepper and serve immediately with plenty of crusty bread.

COOK'S TIP

Sorrel is a large-leafed herb with a slightly sour, lemony flavour that goes very well with fish. It is increasingly easy to find in larger supermarkets, but is also incredibly easy to grow, as a plant.

Basque Tuna Stew

Although versions of this stew are eaten throughout Spain, it originated in the Basque region and would have been largely prepared and eaten by fishermen.

Serves 4

INGREDIENTS

- 5 tbsp olive oil
- 1 large onion, chopped
- 2 garlic cloves, chopped
- 200 g/7 oz can chopped tomatoes
- 700 g/1 lb 9 oz potatoes, cut into 5 cm/2 inch chunks
- 3 green (bell) peppers, deseeded and roughly chopped
- 300 ml/½ pint/ 1¼ cups cold water
- 900 g/2 lb fresh tuna, cut into chunks
- 4 slices crusty white bread
- salt and pepper

1 Heat 2 tablespoons of the oil in a saucepan and add the onion. Cook for 8–10 minutes until soft and brown. Add the garlic and cook a further minute. Add the tomatoes, cover and simmer for 30 minutes until thickened.

2 Meanwhile, in a clean saucepan, mix together the potatoes and peppers. Add the water (which should just cover the vegetables). Bring to the boil and simmer for 15 minutes until the potatoes are almost tender.

3 Add the tuna and the tomato mixture to the potatoes and peppers and season. Cover and simmer for 6–8 minutes until the tuna is tender.

4 Meanwhile, heat the remaining oil in a large frying pan (skillet) over a medium heat and add the bread slices. Fry on both sides until golden. Drain on paper towels. Serve with the stew.

VARIATION

Substitute any very firm-fleshed fish, such as shark or swordfish for the tuna used in this recipe.

Goan Fish Curry

Goan cuisine is famous for seafood dishes and vindaloo dishes, which tend to be very hot. This is a mild dish, but very flavourful.

Serves 4

INGREDIENTS

- 750 g/1½ lb monkfish fillet, cut into chunks
- 1 tbsp cider vinegar
- 1 tsp salt
- 1 tsp ground turmeric
- 3 tbsp vegetable oil
- 2 garlic cloves, crushed
- 1 small onion, finely chopped
- 2 tsp ground coriander
- 1 tsp cayenne pepper
- 2 tsp paprika
- 2 tbsp tamarind pulp plus 2 tbsp boiling water (see method)
- 80 g/3 oz creamed coconut, cut into pieces
- 300 ml/½ pint/1¼ cups warm water
- plain boiled rice, to serve

1 Put the fish on a plate and drizzle over the vinegar. Mix together half the salt and half the turmeric and sprinkle evenly over the fish. Cover and set aside for 20 minutes.

2 Heat the oil in a frying pan (skillet) and add the garlic. Brown slightly then add the onion and fry for 3–4 minutes until soft, but not browned. Add the ground coriander and stir for 1 minute.

3 Mix the remaining turmeric, cayenne and paprika with about 2 tablespoons water to make a paste. Add this to the pan and cook over a low heat for 1–2 minutes.

4 Mix the tamarind pulp with the 2 tablespoons boiling water and stir well. When the water appears thick and the pulp has come away from the seeds, pass this mixture through a sieve, rubbing the pulp well, discard seeds once finished.

5 Add the coconut, warm water and tamarind paste to the pan and stir until the coconut has dissolved. Add the pieces of fish and any juices on the plate and simmer gently for 4–5 minutes until the sauce has thickened and the fish is just tender. Serve immediately on a bed of plain boiled rice.

1

4

5

Thai Green Fish Curry

This pale green curry paste can be used as the basis for all sorts of Thai dishes. It is also delicious with chicken and beef.

Serves 4

INGREDIENTS

- 2 tbsp vegetable oil
- 1 garlic clove, chopped
- 1 small aubergine (eggplant), diced
- 120 ml/4 fl oz/1/2 cup coconut cream
- 2 tbsp Thai fish sauce
- 1 tsp sugar
- 225 g/8 oz firm white fish, cut into pieces, such as cod, haddock, halibut
- 120 ml/4 fl oz/1/2 cup fish stock
- 2 lime leaves, finely shredded
- about 15 leaves Thai basil, if available, or ordinary basil
- plain boiled rice or noodles, to serve

GREEN CURRY PASTE:

- 5 fresh green chillies, deseeded and chopped
- 2 tsp chopped lemon grass
- 1 large shallot, chopped
- 2 garlic cloves, chopped
- 1 tsp freshly grated ginger or galangal, if available
- 2 coriander roots, chopped
- 1/2 tsp ground coriander
- 1/4 tsp ground cumin
- 1 kaffir lime leaf, finely chopped
- 1 tsp shrimp paste (optional)
- 1/2 tsp salt

1 Make the curry paste. Put all the ingredients into a blender or spice grinder and blend to a smooth paste, adding a little water if necessary. Alternatively, pound the ingredients, using a mortar and pestle, until smooth. Set aside.

2 In a frying pan (skillet) or wok, heat the oil until almost smoking and add the garlic. Fry until golden. Add the curry paste and stir-fry a few seconds before adding the aubergine (eggplant). Stir-fry for about 4–5 minutes until softened.

3 Add the coconut cream. Bring to the boil and stir until the cream thickens and curdles slightly. Add the fish sauce and sugar to the frying pan (skillet) and stir well in to the mixture.

4 Add the fish pieces and stock. Simmer for 3–4 minutes, stirring occasionally, until the fish is just tender. Add the lime leaves and basil, and then cook for a further minute. Remove from the frying pan (skillet) or serve with plain boiled rice or noodles.

Mackerel Escabeche

Although the word escabeche is Spanish in origin, variations of this dish are cooked all over the Mediterranean.

Serves 4

INGREDIENTS

- 150 ml/5 fl oz/$\frac{2}{3}$ cup olive oil
- 4 mackerel, filleted
- 2 tbsp seasoned flour, for dusting
- 4 tbsp red wine vinegar
- 1 onion, finely sliced
- 1 strip orange rind, removed with a potato peeler
- 1 sprig fresh thyme
- 1 sprig fresh rosemary
- 1 fresh bay leaf
- 4 garlic cloves, crushed
- 2 fresh red chillies, bruised
- 1 tsp salt
- 3 tbsp chopped fresh flat-leaf parsley
- crusty bread, to serve

1 Heat half the oil in a frying pan (skillet) and dust the mackerel fillets with the seasoned flour.

2 Add the fish to the frying pan and cook for about 30 seconds each side until not quite cooked through.

3 Transfer the mackerel to a shallow dish, large enough to hold the fillets in one layer.

4 Add the the vinegar, onion, orange rind, thyme, rosemary, garlic, chillies and salt to the pan. Simmer for 10 minutes.

5 Add the remaining olive oil and the chopped parsley. Pour the mixture over the fish and leave until cold. Serve with plenty of crusty bread.

VARIATION

Substitute 12 whole sardines, cleaned, with heads removed. Cook in the same way. Tuna steaks are also very delicious served escabeche.

1

2

5

Lemon Sole in a Sweet & Sour Sauce

This is a popular way to serve fish in the Middle East. The fish is first deep-fried and is then served with a delicious sauce of onions, tomatoes, nuts and parsley.

Serves 4

INGREDIENTS

2 large lemon sole, filleted
flour, to dredge
olive oil, to deep-fry plus 2 tbsp olive oil
2 onions, sliced thinly
115 g/4 oz hazelnuts, chopped
50 g/$1\frac{3}{4}$ oz pine kernels (nuts)
50 g/$1\frac{3}{4}$ oz raisins
225 g/8 oz ripe tomatoes, skinned and chopped
2 tbsp red wine vinegar
150 ml/5 fl oz/$\frac{2}{3}$ cup water
3 tbsp chopped fresh parsley
salt and pepper
boiled new potatoes, to serve

1 Wash and dry the fish fillets. Dredge lightly with flour. In a large frying pan (skillet), heat about 2.5 cm/1 inch of olive oil – enough to just cover the fish – over a medium-high heat. Add the fish fillets, 2 at a time, and completely submerge in the oil. Cook for 5–6 minutes then drain on paper towels. Set aside. Cook the remaining fish the same way.

2 Heat the remaining 2 tablespoons of olive oil in a large saucepan. Add the onions and cook for 7–8 minutes until soft and starting to brown. Add the hazelnuts, pine kernels (nuts) and raisins and fry for a further 1–2 minutes until the nuts are golden. Add the tomatoes and cook for 5 minutes until softened.

3 Add the vinegar and simmer for 5 minutes. Add the water, parsley and seasoning and stir well. Simmer a further 5 minutes.

4 Lower the fried fish into the sauce and simmer gently for 10 minutes. Serve with boiled new potatoes.

COOK'S TIP

In the Middle East, many different types of fish are treated this way, but a particular favourite is red mullet. Small fish can be left whole (after cleaning and scaling).

Haddock Baked in Yogurt

This is a very simple dish using store cupboard ingredients.

Serves 4

INGREDIENTS

2 large onions, thinly sliced
900 g/2 lb haddock fillet, from the head end
425 ml/15 fl oz/scant 2 cups natural yogurt
2 tbsp lemon juice
1 tsp sugar
2 tsp ground cumin
2 tsp ground coriander
pinch garam masala
pinch cayenne pepper, to taste
1 tsp freshly grated ginger root
3 tbsp vegetable oil
50 g/1¾ oz/¼ cup cold unsalted butter, cut into pieces
salt and pepper

1 Line a large baking dish with the onion slices. Cut the fish into strips widthways and lay the fish in a single layer over the onions.

2 In a bowl, mix together the yogurt, lemon juice, sugar, cumin, coriander, garam masala, cayenne, ginger, oil and seasoning. Pour this sauce over the fish, making sure it goes under the fish as well. Cover tightly.

3 Bake in a preheated oven at 190°C/375°F/Gas Mark 5 for 30 minutes or until the fish is just tender.

4 Carefully pour the sauce off the fish into a saucepan. Bring to the boil and simmer to reduce the sauce to about 350 ml/12 fl oz/ 1½ fl cups. Remove from the heat.

5 Add the cubes of butter to the sauce and whisk until melted and incorporated. Pour the sauce back over the fish and serve.

COOK'S TIP

When you pour the sauce off the fish it will look thin and separated, but reducing and stirring in the butter will help to amalgamate it.

1

2

4

Cod Italienne

Not strictly authentic, but this dish uses the typical Italian ingredients of tomatoes, capers, olives and basil to make a delicious supper dish.

Serves 4

INGREDIENTS

- 2 tbsp olive oil
- 1 onion, finely chopped
- 2 garlic clove, finely chopped
- 2 tsp freshly chopped thyme
- 150 ml/5 fl oz/⅔ cup red wine
- 2 x 400 g/14 oz cans chopped tomatoes
- pinch sugar
- 50 g/1¾ oz/¼ cup pitted black olives, roughly chopped
- 50 g/1¾ oz/¼ cup pitted green olives, roughly chopped
- 2 tbsp capers, drained, rinsed and roughly chopped
- 2 tbsp chopped fresh basil
- 4 cod steaks, each weighing about 175 g/6 oz
- 150 g/5½ oz ball buffalo Mozzarella, drained and sliced
- salt and pepper
- buttered noodles, to serve

1 Heat the olive oil in a large saucepan. Add the onion and fry gently for 5 minutes until softened but not coloured. Add the garlic and thyme and cook a further minute.

2 Add the red wine and increase the heat. Simmer until reduced and syrupy. Add the tomatoes and sugar and bring to the boil. Cover and simmer for 30 minutes. Uncover and simmer a further 20 minutes until thick. Stir in the olives, capers and basil. Season to taste.

3 Arrange the cod steaks in a shallow ovenproof dish (a lasagne dish is perfect) and spoon the tomato sauce over the top. Bake in a preheated oven at 190°C/375°F/Gas Mark 5 for 20–25 minutes, until the fish is just tender.

4 Remove from the oven and arrange the Mozzarella slices on top of the fish.

5 Return to the oven for a further 5–10 minutes until the cheese has melted. Serve immediately with buttered noodles.

VARIATION

Other white fish steaks would work equally well and, if you want to push the boat out, try turbot.

Cod Curry

Although not strictly authentic, the use of curry paste in this recipe makes it quick and easy to prepare.

Serves 4

INGREDIENTS

- 1 tbsp vegetable oil
- 1 small onion, chopped
- 2 garlic cloves, chopped
- 2.5 cm/1 inch piece fresh ginger root, roughly chopped
- 2 large ripe tomatoes, skinned and roughly chopped
- 150 ml/5 fl oz/⅔ cup fish stock
- 1 tbsp medium curry paste
- 1 tsp ground coriander
- 400 g/14 oz can chick-peas, drained and rinsed
- 750 g/1½ lb cod fillet, cut into large chunks
- 4 tbsp chopped fresh coriander
- 4 tbsp thick yogurt
- salt and pepper
- steamed basmati rice, to serve

1 Heat the oil in a large saucepan and add the onion, garlic and ginger. Fry for 4–5 minutes until softened. Remove from the heat. Put the onion mixture into a food processor or blender with the tomatoes and fish stock and blend until smooth.

2 Return to the saucepan with the curry paste, ground coriander and chick-peas. Mix together well then simmer gently for 15 minutes until thickened.

3 Add the pieces of fish and return to a simmer. Cook for 5 minutes until the fish is just tender. Remove from the heat and leave to stand for 2–3 minutes.

4 Stir in the coriander and yogurt. Season and serve with steamed basmati rice.

VARIATIONS

Instead of cod, make this curry using raw prawns (shrimp) and omit chick-peas.

Home-salted Cod with Chick-peas

You will need to begin preparing this dish two days ahead to allow for salting the cod.

Serves 6

INGREDIENTS

50 g/1¾ oz sea salt1.5 kg/3 lb 5oz fresh boneless cod fillet, from the head end, skin on
225 g/8 oz dried chick-peas, soaked overnight
1 fresh red chilli
4 garlic cloves
2 bay leaves
1 tbsp olive oil
300 ml/½ pint/1¼ cups chicken stock
pepper
extra-virgin olive oil, to drizzle

GREMOLATA:
3 tbsp chopped fresh parsley
2 garlic cloves, finely chopped
finely grated rind of 1 lemon

1 Sprinkle the salt over both sides of the cod fillet. Place in a shallow dish, cover and refrigerate for 48 hours. When ready to cook, remove cod from the refrigerator and rinse under cold water. Leave to soak in cold water for 2 hours.

2 Drain the chick-peas, rinse them thoroughly and drain again. Put into a large saucepan. Add double their volume of water and bring slowly to the boil. Remove any scum that rises to the surface. Split the chilli lengthways and add to the chick-peas with the whole garlic cloves and bay leaves. Cover and simmer for 1½–2 hours until very tender, skimming occasionally if necessary.

3 Drain the cod and pat dry. Brush with the olive oil and season well with black pepper (but no salt). Cook under a preheated grill (broiler) or on a hot ridged grill pan for 3–4 minutes on each side until tender. Meanwhile, add the chicken stock to the chick-peas and bring back to the boil. Keep warm.

4 For the gremolata, mix together the parsley, garlic and finely grated lemon rind.

5 To serve, ladle the chick-peas and their cooking liquid into 6 warmed soup bowls. Top with the grilled (broiled) cod and sprinkle over the gremolata. Drizzle generously with olive oil and serve.

Cotriade

This is a rich French stew of fish and vegetables, flavoured with saffron and herbs. Traditionally, the fish and vegetables, and the soup, are served separately.

Serves 6

INGREDIENTS

large pinch saffron
600 ml/1 pint/2½ cups hot fish stock
1 tbsp olive oil
25 g/1 oz/2 tbsp butter
1 onion, sliced
2 garlic cloves, chopped
1 leek, sliced
1 small fennel bulb, finely sliced
450 g/1 lb potatoes, cut into chunks
150 ml/5 fl oz/⅔ cup dry white wine
1 tbsp fresh thyme leaves
2 bay leaves
4 ripe tomatoes, skinned and chopped
900 g/2 lb mixed fish such as haddock, hake, mackerel, red or grey mullet, roughly chopped
2 tbsp chopped fresh parsley
salt and pepper
crusty bread, to serve

1 Using a mortar and pestle, crush the saffron and add to the fish stock. Stir and leave to infuse for at least 10 minutes.

2 In a large saucepan, heat the oil and butter together. Add the onion and cook gently for 4–5 minutes until softened. Add the garlic, leek, fennel and potatoes. Cover and cook for a further 10–15 minutes until the vegetables are softened.

3 Add the wine and simmer rapidly for 3–4 minutes until reduced by half. Add the thyme, bay leaves and tomatoes and stir well. Add the saffron-infused fish stock. Bring to the boil, cover and simmer gently for 15 minutes until the vegetables are tender.

4 Add the fish, return to the boil and simmer for a further 3–4 minutes until all the fish is tender. Add the parsley and season to taste. Using a slotted spoon, remove the fish and vegetables to a warmed serving dish. Serve the soup with plenty of crusty bread.

VARIATION

Once the fish and vegetables have been cooked, the soup could be liquidised and passed through a sieve to give a smooth fish soup.

1

2

4

Squid Stew

This is a rich and flavourful stew of slowly cooked squid, in a sauce of tomatoes and red wine. The squid becomes very tender.

Serves 4

INGREDIENTS

750 g/1 lb 10 oz squid
3 tbsp olive oil
1 onion, chopped
3 garlic cloves, finely chopped
1 tsp fresh thyme leaves
400 g/14 oz can chopped tomatoes
150 ml/5 fl oz/$^{2}/_{3}$ cup red wine
300 ml/$^{1}/_{2}$ pint/1$^{1}/_{4}$ cups water
1 tbsp chopped fresh parsley
salt and pepper

1 To prepare whole squid, hold the body firmly and grasp the tentacles just inside the body. Pull firmly to remove the innards. Find the transparent 'backbone' and remove. Grasp the wings on the outside of the body and pull to remove the outer skin. Trim the tentacles just below the beak and reserve. Wash the body and tentacles under running water. Slice the body into rings. Drain well on paper towels.

2 Heat the oil in a large, flameproof casserole. Add the prepared squid and cook over a medium heat, stirring occasionally, until lightly browned.

3 Reduce the heat and add the onion, garlic and thyme. Cook a further 5 minutes until softened.

4 Stir in the tomatoes, red wine and water. Bring to the boil and cook to a preheated oven at 140°C/275°F/Gas Mark 1 for 2 hours. Stir in the parsley and season to taste.

VARIATIONS

This stew can be used as the basis for a more substantial fish stew. Before adding the parsley, add extra seafood such as scallops, pieces of fish fillet, large prawns (jumbo shrimp) or even cooked lobster. Return the stew to the boil and cook a further 2 minutes. Add the parsley and seasoning.

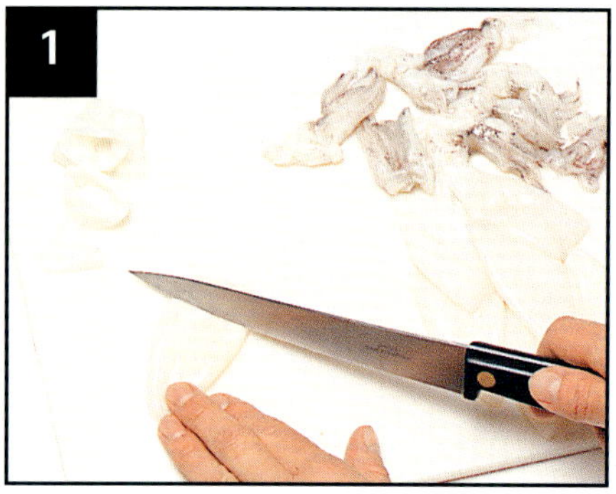

Spanish Fish Stew

This is an impressive-looking Catalan dish using two classic Spanish cooking methods – the sofrito, a slow-cooked mixture of vegetables, and the picada, usually nuts, bread and garlic, used to finish and thicken the stew.

Serves 6

INGREDIENTS

- 5 tbsp olive oil
- 2 large onions, finely chopped
- 2 ripe tomatoes, skinned, deseeded and diced
- 2 slices white bread, crusts removed
- 4 almonds, toasted
- 3 garlic cloves, roughly chopped
- 350 g/12 oz cooked lobster
- 200 g/7 oz cleaned squid
- 200 g/7 oz monkfish fillet
- 200 g/7 oz cod fillet, skinned
- 1 tbsp plain (all purpose) flour
- 6 large raw prawns (jumbo shrimp)
- 6 langoustines
- 18 live mussels, scrubbed, beards removed
- 8 large live clams, scrubbed
- 1 tbsp chopped fresh parsley
- 120 ml/4 fl oz/½ cup brandy
- salt and pepper

1 Heat 3 tablespoons of the oil in a frying pan (skillet), add the onions and cook gently for 10–15 minutes until lightly golden, adding a little water to prevent them sticking, if necessary. Add the tomatoes and cook until they have melted down and the oil has separated away from them.

2 Heat 1 tablespoon of the remaining oil and fry the slices of bread until crisp. Break into rough pieces and put into a mortar with the almonds and 2 garlic cloves. Pound together to make a fine paste. Alternatively, blend to a paste in a food processor.

3 To prepare the lobster, split it lengthways. Remove and discard the intestinal vein which runs down the tail, the stomach sac and the spongy-looking gills. Crack the claws and remove the meat. Take out the flesh from the tail and chop into large chunks. Slice the squid into rings.

4 Season the monkfish, cod and lobster and dust with a little flour. In a frying pan (skillet), heat a little of the remaining oil and brown the fish separately: monkfish, cod, lobster, then squid, prawns and langoustines. Arrange them in a flameproof casserole as they brown.

5 Add the mussels and clams to the browned fish. Add the remaining garlic and parsley and place the pan over a low heat. Pour over the brandy and ignite. When the flames have died down, add the tomato mixture and just enough water to cover. Bring to the boil and simmer for 3–4 minutes until the mussels and clams have opened. Discard any that remain closed. Stir in the bread mixture and season to taste. Simmer a further 5 minutes until all the fish is tender.

Moroccan Fish Tagine

A tagine is a Moroccan cooking vessel consisting of an earthenware dish with a domed lid that has a steam hole in the top. However, this dish can be made quite successfully in an ordinary pan.

Serves 4

INGREDIENTS

2 tbsp olive oil
1 large onion, finely chopped
large pinch saffron strands
$\frac{1}{2}$ tsp ground cinnamon
1 tsp ground coriander
$\frac{1}{2}$ tsp ground cumin
$\frac{1}{2}$ tsp ground turmeric
200 g/7 oz can chopped tomatoes
300 ml/$\frac{1}{2}$ pint/$1\frac{1}{4}$ cups fish stock
4 small red mullet cleaned, boned and heads and tails removed
50 g/$1\frac{3}{4}$ oz pitted green olives
1 tbsp chopped preserved lemon
3 tbsp fresh chopped coriander
salt and pepper
couscous, to serve

1 Heat the olive oil in a large saucepan or flameproof casserole. Add the onion and cook gently for 10 minutes without colouring until softened. Add the saffron, cinnamon, coriander, cumin and turmeric and cook for a further 30 seconds, stirring.

2 Add the chopped tomatoes and fish stock and stir well. Bring to the boil, cover and simmer for 15 minutes. Uncover and simmer for a further 20–35 minutes until thickened.

3 Cut each red mullet in half then add the pieces to the pan, pushing them into the sauce. Simmer gently for a further 5–6 minutes until the fish is just cooked.

4 Carefully stir in the olives, preserved lemon and the chopped coriander. Season to taste and serve with couscous.

COOK'S TIP

Preserved lemons are simple to make yourself. Take enough lemons to completely fill a preserving jar and quarter them lengthways without cutting all the way through. Pack the lemons with 50 g/$1\frac{3}{4}$ oz/ $\frac{1}{4}$ cup sea salt per lemon, adding any remaining salt to the jar. Add the juice of a further lemon and top up with water to cover. Leave for at least 1 month before using.

Stewed Sardines

This is an unusual stew of sardines cooked with baby onions, tomatoes, olives, raisins, Marsala and pine kernels (nuts).

Serves 4

INGREDIENTS

- 50 g/1 3/4 oz/3/4 cup raisins
- 3 tbsp Marsala
- 4 tbsp olive oil
- 225 g/8 oz baby onions, halved if large
- 2 garlic cloves, chopped
- 1 tbsp chopped fresh sage
- 4 large tomatoes, skinned and chopped
- 150 ml/fl oz/2/3 cup fish or vegetable stock
- 2 tbsp balsamic vinegar
- 450 g/1 lb fresh sardines, cleaned
- 25 g/1 oz pitted black olives
- 25 g/1 oz pine kernels (nuts), toasted
- 2 tbsp chopped fresh parsley

1 Put the raisins in a small bowl and pour over the Marsala. Leave to soak for about 1 hour until the raisins are plump. Strain, reserving both the Marsala and the raisins.

2 Heat the olive oil in a large saucepan and fry the onions over a low heat for 15 minutes until golden and tender. Add the garlic and sage and cook for a further minute. Add the tomatoes, fry for a further 2–3 minutes then add the stock, vinegar and reserved Marsala. Bring to the boil, cover and simmer for 25 minutes.

3 Add the sardines to the stew and simmer gently for 2–3 minutes before adding the raisins, olives and pine kernels (nuts). Simmer for a final 2–3 minutes until the fish are cooked. Add the parsley and serve immediately.

VARIATIONS

Substitute Home-salted Cod (see page 90) or smoked cod for the sardines.

Red Prawn Curry

Like all Thai curries, this one has as its base a paste of chillies and spices and a sauce of coconut milk. If you have access to a Thai supplier, buy the paste ready-made as the Thais do.

Serves 4

INGREDIENTS

2 tbsp vegetable oil
1 garlic clove, finely chopped
1 tbsp red curry paste
200 ml/7 fl oz/scant 1 cup coconut milk
2 tbsp Thai fish sauce
1 tsp sugar
12 large raw prawns, de-veined
2 lime leaves, finely shredded
1 small red chilli, deseeded and finely sliced
10 leaves Thai basil, if available, or ordinary basil

RED CURRY PASTE:
3 dried long red chillies
½ tsp ground coriander
¼ tsp ground cumin
½ tsp ground black pepper
2 garlic cloves, chopped
2 stalks lemon grass, chopped
1 kaffir lime leaf, finely chopped
1 tsp freshly grated ginger root or galangal, if available
1 tsp shrimp paste (optional)
½ tsp salt

1 Make the red curry paste. Put all the ingredients in a blender or spice grinder and blend to a smooth paste, adding a little water if necessary. Alternatively, pound the ingredients using a mortar and pestle until smooth. Set aside.

2 Heat the oil in a wok or frying pan (skillet) until almost smoking. Add the chopped garlic and fry until golden. Add 1 tablespoon of the curry paste and cook for a further minute. Add half the coconut milk, the fish sauce and the sugar. Stir well. The mixture should thicken slightly.

3 Add the prawns and simmer for 3–4 minutes until they turn colour. Add the remaining coconut milk, the lime leaves and the chilli. Cook a further 2–3 minutes until the prawns are just tender.

4 Add the basil leaves, stir until wilted and serve immediately.

COOK'S TIP

This recipe makes a little more curry paste than you need, but it keeps well. Stir a little into canned tuna with some chopped spring onion, lime juice and pinto beans for a delicious sandwich filling.

Curried Prawns with Courgettes (Zucchini)

The best way to approach this recipe is to prepare everything beforehand – including measuring out the spices. The cooking time is then very quick.

Serves 4

INGREDIENTS

350 g/12 oz small courgettes (zucchini)
1 tsp salt
450 g/1 lb cooked tiger prawns (jumbo shrimp)
5 tbsp vegetable oil
4 garlic cloves, finely chopped
5 tbsp chopped fresh coriander
1 fresh green chilli, deseeded and finely chopped
½ tsp ground turmeric
1½ tsp ground cumin
pinch cayenne pepper
200 g/7 oz can chopped tomatoes
1 tsp freshly grated ginger
1 tbsp lemon juice
steamed basmati rice, to serve

1 Wash and trim the courgettes (zucchini). Cut into small batons. Put into a colander and sprinkle with a little of the salt. Set aside for 30 minutes. Rinse, drain and pat dry. Spread the prawns (shrimp) on paper towels to drain.

2 In a wok or frying pan (skillet), heat the oil over a high heat. Add the garlic. As soon as the garlic begins to brown, add the courgettes (zucchini), coriander, green chilli, turmeric, cumin, cayenne, tomatoes, ginger, lemon juice and remaining salt. Stir well and bring to the boil.

3 Cover and simmer over a low heat for about 5 minutes. Uncover and add the prawns.

4 Increase the heat to high and simmer for about 5 minutes to reduce the liquid to a thick sauce. Serve immediately with steamed basmati rice, garnished with lime wedges.

VARIATION

If you can't find cooked tiger prawns (jumbo shrimp) for this recipe, use cooked peeled prawns (shrimp) instead but these release quite a lot of liquid so you may need to increase the final simmering time to thicken the sauce.

1

2

3

Salads, Summer Dishes & Suppers

Fish is the perfect ingredient for a mid-week supper because it cooks so quickly. It is also wonderful marinated and simply grilled or barbecued and makes a perfect ingredient in a salad, either warm or cold.

This chapter contains a variety of recipes designed to be simple but taste as if you have spent hours preparing them. There are substantial main course salads, like Tuna Bean Salad, Moroccan Couscous Salad or Caesar Salad.

Quick suppers include the best Cod & Chips ever, plus Salmon Frittata and Tuna Fishcakes. Lots of barbecue ideas are here as well, including Barbecued Monkfish, Char-grilled Scallops and Mixed Seafood Brochettes.

Caesar Salad

Caesar salad was the invention of a chef at a large hotel in Acapulco, Mexico. It has rightly earned an international reputation.

Serves 4

INGREDIENTS

1 large cos (romaine) lettuce or 2 hearts of romaine
4 anchovies, drained and halved lengthways
Parmesan shavings, to garnish

DRESSING:
2 garlic cloves, crushed
1½ tsp Dijon mustard
1 tsp Worcestershire sauce
4 anchovies in olive oil, drained and chopped
1 egg yolk
1 tbsp lemon juice
150 ml/5 fl oz/⅔ cup olive oil
4 tbsp freshly grated Parmesan cheese
salt and pepper

CROÛTONS:
4 thick slices day-old bread
2 tbsp olive oil
1 garlic clove, crushed

1 Make the dressing. In a food processor or blender, put the garlic, mustard, Worcestershire sauce, anchovies, egg yolk, lemon juice and seasoning and blend together for 30 seconds, until foaming. Add the olive oil, drop by drop until the mixture begins to thicken then in a steady stream until all the oil is incorporated. Scrape out of the food processor or blender. Add a little hot water if the dressing is too thick. Stir in the grated Parmesan cheese. Taste for seasoning and set aside in the refrigerator until required.

2 For the croûtons, cut the bread into 1 cm/½ inch cubes. Toss with the oil and garlic in a bowl. Transfer to a baking sheet (cookie sheet) in a single. Bake in a preheated oven at 180°C/350°F/ Gas Mark 4, for 15–20 minutes, stirring occasionally, until the croûtons are browned and crisp. Remove from the oven and allow to cool. Set aside.

3 Separate the cos (romaine) lettuce or hearts of romaine into individual leaves and wash. Tear into pieces and spin dry in a salad spinner. Alternatively, dry the leaves on clean paper towels (kitchen towels). (Excess moisture will dilute the dressing and make the salad taste watery.) Transfer to a plastic bag and refrigerate until needed.

4 To assemble the salad, put the lettuce pieces into a large serving bowl. Add the dressing and toss thoroughly until all the leaves are coated. Top with the halved anchovies, croûtons and Parmesan shavings. Serve at once while still hot.

Moroccan Couscous Salad

Couscous is a type of fine semolina made from wheat. Traditionally it is steamed over a stew in a special couscousier, which is essentially a large pot with a steamer attachment that sits on the top. Nowadays, you can buy couscous pre-cooked so that it needs only the addition of boiling water.

Serves 4

INGREDIENTS

225 g/8 oz/1 cup couscous
1 cinnamon stick, about 5 cm/2 inches
2 tsp coriander seeds
1 tsp cumin seeds
2 tbsp olive oil
1 small onion, finely chopped
2 garlic cloves, finely chopped
½ tsp ground turmeric
pinch cayenne pepper
1 tbsp lemon juice
50 g/1¾ oz/¼ cup sultanas (golden raisins)
3 ripe plum tomatoes, chopped
80 g/3 oz cucumber, chopped
4 spring onions, sliced
200 g/7 oz can tuna in olive oil, drained and flaked
3 tbsp chopped fresh coriander
salt and pepper

1 Cook the couscous according to the packet instructions, omitting any butter recommended. Transfer to a large bowl and set aside.

2 Heat a small frying pan (skillet) and add the cinnamon stick, coriander seeds and cumin seeds. Cook over a high heat until the seeds begin to pop and smell fragrant. Remove from the heat and pour the seeds into a mortar. Grind with a pestle to a fine powder. Alternatively, grind in a spice grinder. Set aside.

3 Heat the oil in a clean frying pan (skillet) and add the onion. Cook over a low heat for 7–8 minutes until softened and lightly browned. Add the garlic and cook for a further minute. Stir in the roasted and ground spices, turmeric and cayenne and cook for a further minute. Remove from the heat and stir in the lemon juice. Add this mixture to the couscous and mix well together, ensuring that all of the grains are coated.

4 Add the sultanas (golden raisins), tomatoes, cucumber, spring onions, tuna and chopped coriander. Season with salt and pepper to taste and mix together. Allow to cool completely and serve at room temperature.

Tuna Niçoise Salad

This is a classic version of the French Salade Niçoise. It is a substantial salad, suitable for a lunch or light summer supper.

Serves 4

INGREDIENTS

- 4 eggs
- 450 g/1 lb new potatoes
- 115 g/4 oz/1 cup dwarf green beans, trimmed and halved
- 2 x 175 g/6 oz tuna steaks
- 6 tbsp olive oil, plus extra for brushing
- 1 garlic clove, crushed
- 1½ tsp Dijon mustard
- 2 tsp lemon juice
- 2 tbsp chopped fresh basil
- 2 Little Gem lettuces
- 200 g/7 oz/1½ cups cherry tomatoes, halved
- 175 g/6 oz/2 cups cucumber, peeled, cut in half and sliced
- 50 g/1¾ oz/½ cup pitted black olives
- 50 g/1¾ oz can anchovies in oil, drained
- salt and pepper

1 Bring a small saucepan of water to the boil. Add the eggs and cook for 7–9 minutes from when the water returns to the boil – 7 minutes for a slightly soft centre, 9 minutes for a firm centre. Drain and refresh under cold running water. Set aside

2 Cook the potatoes in boiling salted water for 10–12 minutes until tender. Add the beans 3 minutes before the end of the cooking time. Drain both vegetables well and refresh under cold water. Drain well.

3 Wash and dry the tuna steaks. Brush with a little olive oil and season. Cook on a preheated ridged grill pan for 2–3 minutes each side, until just tender but still slightly pink in the centre. Set aside to rest.

4 Whisk together the garlic, mustard, lemon juice, basil and seasoning. Whisk in the olive oil.

5 To assemble the salad, break apart the lettuces and tear into large pieces. Divide between individual serving plates. Next add the potatoes and beans, tomatoes, cucumber and olives. Toss lightly together. Shell the eggs and cut into quarters lengthways. Arrange these on top of the salad. Scatter over the anchovies.

6 Flake the tuna steaks and arrange on the salads. Pour over the dressing and serve.

3

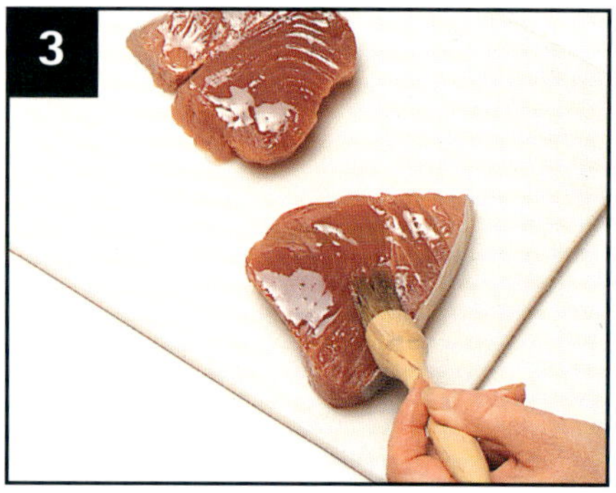

5

VARIATION

Use 2 x 200 g/7 oz cans of tuna in olive oil, drained and flaked, instead of the fresh tuna.

Tuna Bean Salad

Don't panic if you forget to soak the dried beans overnight. Place them in a saucepan with plenty of water, bring to the boil, turn off the heat and leave to soak, covered, for at least 2 hours.

Serves 4

INGREDIENTS

- 225 g/8 oz/1 cup dried haricot (navy) beans
- 1 tbsp lemon juice
- 5 tbsp extra-virgin olive oil, plus extra for brushing
- 1 garlic clove, finely chopped
- 1 small red onion, very finely sliced (optional)
- 1 tbsp chopped fresh parsley
- 4 x 175 g/6 oz tuna steaks
- salt and pepper

TO GARNISH:
- parsley sprigs
- lemon wedges

1 Soak the haricot beans for 8 hours or overnight in at least twice their volume of cold water.

2 When you're ready to cook, drain the beans and place in a saucepan with twice their volume of fresh water. Bring slowly to the boil, skimming off any scum that rises to the surface. Boil the beans rapidly for 10 minutes, then reduce the heat and simmer for a further 1¼–1½ hours until the beans are tender.

3 Meanwhile, mix together the lemon juice, olive oil, garlic and seasoning. Drain the beans thoroughly and mix together with the olive oil mixture, onion and parsley. Season to taste and set aside.

4 Wash and dry the tuna steaks. Brush lightly with olive oil and season. Cook on a preheated ridged grill pan for 2 minutes on each side until just pink in the centre.

5 Divide the bean salad between 4 serving plates. Top each with a tuna steak. Garnish with parsley sprigs and lemon wedges and serve immediately.

COOK'S TIP

You could use canned haricot (navy) beans instead of dried. Reheat according to the instructions on the can, drain and toss with the dressing as above.

1

4

5

Thai Seafood Salad

This salad is best served chilled.

Serves 4

INGREDIENTS

450 g/1 lb live mussels
8 raw tiger prawns (jumbo shrimp)
350 g/12 oz squid, cleaned and sliced widthways into rings
115 g/4 oz cooked peeled prawns (shrimp)
½ red onion, finely sliced
½ red (bell) pepper, deseeded and finely sliced
115 g/4 oz/1 cup bean-sprouts
115 g/4 oz/2 cups shredded pak choy (Chinese leaves)

DRESSING:
1 garlic clove, crushed
1 tsp grated fresh ginger root
1 red chilli, deseeded and finely chopped
2 tbsp chopped fresh coriander
1 tbsp lime juice
1 tsp finely grated lime rind
1 tbsp light soy sauce
5 tbsp sunflower or groundnut oil
2 tsp sesame oil
salt and pepper

1 Prepare the mussels by scrubbing or scraping the shells and removing any beards. Place in a large saucepan with just the water that clings to their shells. Cook over a high heat for 3–4 minutes, shaking the pan occasionally, until all the mussels have opened. Discard any that remain closed. Strain the mussels, reserving the poaching liquid, and refresh the mussels under cold water. Drain again and set aside.

2 Bring the reserved poaching liquid to the boil and add the tiger prawns (shrimp). Simmer for 5 minutes. Add the squid and cook for a further 2 minutes until both the prawns (shrimp) and squid are cooked through. Remove them with a slotted spoon and plunge immediately into a large bowl of cold water. Reserve the poaching liquid. Drain the prawns (shrimp) and squid again.

3 Remove the mussels from their shells and put into a bowl with the tiger prawns (shrimp), squid and cooked peeled prawns (shrimp). Refrigerate for 1 hour.

4 For the dressing, put all the ingredients, except the oils, into a blender or spice grinder and blend to a smooth paste. Add the oils, reserved poaching liquid, seasoning and 4 tbsp cold water. Blend again to combine.

5 Just before serving, combine the onion, red (bell) pepper, bean-sprouts and pak choy in a bowl and toss with 2–3 tbsp of the dressing. Arrange the vegetables on a large serving plate or in a bowl. Toss the remaining dressing with the seafood to coat and add to the vegetables. Serve at once.

3

5

Skate & Spinach Salad

This salad makes a filling main course or would serve six as a starter. Fresh skate should have a faint smell of ammonia; if the smell is very strong, do not use the fish.

Serves 4

INGREDIENTS

- 700 g/1 lb 9 oz skate wings, trimmed
- 2 sprigs fresh rosemary
- 1 fresh bay leaf
- 1 tbsp black peppercorns
- 1 lemon, quartered
- 450 g/1 lb baby spinach leaves
- 1 tbsp olive oil
- 1 small red onion, thinly sliced
- 2 garlic cloves, crushed
- ½ tsp chilli flakes
- 50 g/1¾ oz pine kernels (nuts), lightly toasted
- 50 g/1¾ oz raisins
- 1 tbsp light muscovado (brown) sugar
- 2 tbsp chopped fresh parsley

1 Put the skate wings into a large saucepan with the rosemary, bay leaf, peppercorns and lemon quarters. Cover with cold water and bring to the boil. Simmer, covered, for 4–5 minutes until the flesh begins to come away from the cartilage. Remove from the heat and leave for 15 minutes.

2 Lift the fish from the poaching water and remove the flesh from the fish in shreds. Set aside.

3 Meanwhile, in a clean saucepan, cook the spinach with just the water that clings to the leaves after washing, over a high heat for 30 seconds until just wilted. Drain, refresh under cold water and drain well once more. Squeeze out any excess water and set aside.

4 Heat the olive oil in a large, deep frying pan (skillet). Add the red onion and fry for 3–4 minutes until softened but not browned. Add the garlic, chilli flakes, pine kernels (nuts), raisins and sugar. Cook for 1–2 minutes, then add the spinach and toss for 1 minute until heated through.

5 Gently fold in the skate and cook for a further minute. Season well.

6 Divide the salad between 4 serving plates and sprinkle with the chopped parsley. Serve immediately.

1

2

4

Grilled Red Mullet

Try to get small red mullet for this dish. If you can only get larger fish, serve one to each person and increase the cooking time accordingly.

Serves 4

INGREDIENTS

1 lemon, thinly sliced
2 garlic cloves, crushed
4 sprigs fresh flat-leaf parsley
4 sprigs fresh thyme
8 leaves fresh sage
2 large shallots, sliced
8 small red mullet, cleaned
8 slices Parma ham (prosciutto)
salt and pepper

SAUTE POTATOES AND SHALLOTS:
4 tbsp olive oil
900 g/2 lb potatoes, diced
8 whole garlic cloves, unpeeled
12 small whole shallots

FOR THE DRESSING:
4 tbsp olive oil
1 tbsp lemon juice
1 tbsp chopped fresh flat-leaf parsley
1 tbsp chopped fresh chives
salt and pepper

1 For the sauté potatoes and shallots, heat the olive oil in a large frying pan (skillet) and add the potatoes, garlic cloves and shallots. Cook gently, stirring regularly, for 12–15 minutes until golden, crisp and tender.

2 Meanwhile, divide the lemon slices, halved if necessary, garlic, parsley, thyme, sage and shallots between the cavities of the fish. Season well. Wrap a slice of Parma ham (prosciutto) around each fish. Secure with a cocktail stick (toothpick).

3 Arrange fish on a grill (broiler) pan and cook under a preheated hot grill (broiler) for 5–6 minutes on each side until tender.

4 To make the dressing, mix together the oil and lemon juice with the finely chopped parsley and chives. Season to taste.

5 Divide the potatoes and shallots between 4 serving plates and top each with the fish. Drizzle around the dressing and serve immediately.

Poached Rainbow Trout

As this is served cold, it makes a lovely summer lunch or supper dish.

Serves 4

INGREDIENTS

4 x 375 g/12 oz rainbow trout, cleaned
700 g/1 lb 9 oz new potatoes
3 spring onions (scallions), finely chopped
1 egg, hard-boiled (hard-cooked) and chopped

COURT-BOUILLON:
850 ml/1½ pints/3¾ cups cold water
850 ml/1½ pints/3¾ cups dry white wine
3 tbsp white wine vinegar
2 large carrots, roughly chopped
1 onion, roughly chopped
2 celery sticks, roughly chopped
2 leeks, roughly chopped
2 garlic cloves, roughly chopped
2 fresh bay leaves
4 sprigs fresh parsley
4 sprigs fresh thyme
6 black peppercorns
1 tsp salt

WATERCRESS MAYONNAISE:
1 egg yolk
1 tsp Dijon mustard
1 tsp white wine vinegar
50 g/2 oz watercress leaves, chopped
225 ml/8 fl oz/1 cup light olive oil
salt and pepper

1 First make the court-bouillon. Place all the ingredients in a large saucepan and bring slowly to the boil. Cover and simmer gently for about 30 minutes. Strain the liquid through a fine sieve into a clean pan. Bring to the boil again and simmer fast, uncovered, for 15–20 minutes until the court-bouillon is reduced to 600 ml/1 pint/2½ cups.

2

2 Place the trout in a large frying pan (skillet). Add the court-bouillon and bring slowly to the boil. Remove from the heat and leave the fish in the poaching liquid to go cold.

3 Meanwhile, make the watercress mayonnaise. Put the egg yolk, mustard, wine vinegar, watercress and seasoning into a food processor or blender and blend for 30 seconds until foaming. Begin adding the olive oil, drop by drop, until the mixture begins to thicken. Continue adding the oil in a slow steady stream until it is all incorporated. Add a little hot water if the mixture seems too thick. Season to taste and set aside.

4 Cook the potatoes in plenty of boiling salted water for 12–15 minutes until soft and tender. Drain well and refresh them under cold running water. Set the potatoes aside until cold.

5 When the potatoes are cold, cut them in half if they are very large, and toss thoroughly with the watercress mayonnaise, finely chopped spring onions (scallions) and hard-boiled (hard-cooked) egg.

6 Carefully lift the fish from the poaching liquid and drain on paper towels. Carefully pull the skin away from each of the trout and serve immediately with the potato salad.

Baked Salmon

This is a wonderful dish to serve as part of a buffet lunch or supper and can be served hot or cold.

Serves 8–10

INGREDIENTS

3 kg/6 lb 8 oz salmon filleted
8 tbsp chopped mixed herbs
2 tbsp green peppercorns in brine, drained
1 tsp finely grated lime rind
6 tbsp dry vermouth or dry white wine
salt and pepper
parsley sprigs, to garnish

RED (BELL) PEPPER RELISH:
120 ml/4 fl oz/½ cup white wine vinegar
300 ml/10 fl oz/¼ cups light olive oil
1–2 tsp chilli sauce, to taste
6 spring onions (scallions), finely sliced
1 orange or red (bell) pepper, deseeded and finely diced
1 tbsp chopped fresh flat-leaf parsley
2 tbsp chopped fresh chives

CAPER AND GHERKIN MAYONNAISE:
350 ml/12 fl oz/1½ cups good quality mayonnaise
3 tbsp chopped capers
3 tbsp finely chopped gherkins
2 tbsp chopped fresh flat-leaf parsley
1 tbsp Dijon mustard

1 Wash and dry the salmon fillets and place one fillet, skin side down, on a large sheet of oiled foil. Mix together the herbs, peppercorns and lime rind and spread over the top. Season well and lay the second fillet on top, skin side up. Drizzle over the vermouth or white wine. Wrap the foil over the salmon, twisting well to make a loose but tightly sealed parcel.

2 Transfer the foil parcel to a large baking sheet (cookie sheet) and bake in a preheated oven at 120/C°250°F/Gas Mark ½, for 1½ hours until tender. Remove from the oven and allow to rest for 20 minutes before serving.

3 Meanwhile, make the red (bell) pepper relish. Whisk together the vinegar, olive oil and chilli sauce to taste. Add the spring onions (scallions), red (bell) pepper, parsley and chives. Season and set aside.

4 To make the caper and gherkin mayonnaise, mix all the ingredients together and set aside.

5 Unwrap the cooked salmon and slice thickly. Arrange the slices on a large serving platter and serve with the red (bell) pepper relish and caper and gherkin mayonnaise. Garnish with fresh parsley sprigs.

Barbecued Monkfish

Monkfish cooks very well on a barbecue because it is a firm-fleshed fish.

Serves 4

INGREDIENTS

4 tbsp olive oil
grated rind of 1 lime
2 tsp Thai fish sauce
2 garlic cloves, crushed
1 tsp grated fresh ginger root
2 tbsp chopped fresh basil
700 g/1 lb 9 oz monkfish fillet, cut into chunks
2 limes, each cut into 6 wedges
salt and pepper

1 Mix together the olive oil, lime rind, fish sauce, garlic, ginger and basil. Season and set aside.

2 Wash the dry the fish. Add to the marinade and mix well. Leave to marinate for 2 hours, stirring occasionally.

3 If you are using bamboo skewers, soak them in cold water for 30 minutes. Then, lift the monkfish pieces from the marinade and thread them on to the skewers, alternating with the lime wedges.

4 Transfer the skewers, either to a lit barbecue or to a preheated ridged grill pan. Cook for 5–6 minutes, turning regularly, until the fish is tender. Serve immediately.

VARIATION

You could use any type of white fleshed fish for this recipe but sprinkle the pieces with salt and leave for 2 hours to firm the flesh, before rinsing, drying and then adding to the marinade.

2

3

4

Cod & Chips

This is the genuine article. A crunchy, deep golden batter surrounding perfectly cooked fish, served with golden crispy chips. If you've never had chips with mayonnaise, try them with this lovely mustardy version and you'll be converted.

Serves 4

INGREDIENTS

900 g/2 lb old potatoes
4 x 175 g/6 oz thick pieces cod fillet, preferably from the head end
vegetable oil, for deep-frying
salt and pepper

BATTER:
15 g/½ oz fresh yeast
300 ml/½ pint/1¼ cups beer
225 g/8 oz/2 cups plain flour
2 tsp salt

MAYONNAISE:
1 egg yolk
1 tsp wholegrain mustard
1 tbsp lemon juice
200 ml/7 fl oz/1 cup light olive oil
salt and pepper

TO GARNISH:
lemon wedges
parsley sprigs

1 For the batter, cream the yeast with a little of the beer to a smooth paste. Gradually stir in the rest of the beer. Sift the plain (all-purpose) flour and salt into a bowl, make a well in the centre and add the yeast mixture. Gradually whisk to a smooth batter. Cover and leave at room temperature for 1 hour.

2 For the mayonnaise, put the egg yolk, mustard, lemon juice and seasoning into a food processor. Blend for 30 seconds until frothy. Begin adding the olive oil, drop by drop, until the mixture begins to thicken. Continue adding the oil in a slow, steady stream until all the oil has been incorporated. Taste for seasoning. Thin with a little hot water if the mayonnaise is too thick. Refrigerate until needed.

4

3 For the fish and chips, cut the potatoes into chips about 1.5 cm/½ inch thick. Heat a large saucepan half filled with vegetable oil to 140°C/275°F or until a cube of bread browns in 1 minute. Cook the chips in 2 batches for about 5 minutes, until they are cooked through but not browned. Place the chips to drain on paper towels and set aside.

4 Increase the heat to 160°C/325°F or until a cube of bread browns in 45 seconds. Season the fish then dip into the batter. Fry 2 pieces at a time for 7–8 minutes until deep golden brown and cooked through. Drain on paper towels and keep warm while you cook remaining fish. Keep these warm while you finish cooking the chips.

5 Increase the heat to 190°C/375°F or until a cube of bread browns in 30 seconds. Fry the chips again, in 2 batches, for 2–3 minutes until crisp and golden. Drain on paper and sprinkle with salt.

6 Serve the fish with the chips and mayonnaise. Serve while still hot garnished with lemon wedges and parsley sprigs.

Haddock Goujons

Focaccia is an Italian flat bread made with plenty of olive oil. It may include other flavourings as well, including herbs, sun-dried tomatoes and olives. It is widely available in large supermarkets.

Serves 4

INGREDIENTS

175 g/6 oz herb focaccia bread
700 g/1 lb 9 oz skinless, boneless haddock fillet
2–3 tbsp plain (all-purpose) flour
2 eggs, lightly beaten
vegetable oil, for deep-frying
lemon wedges, to serve
parsley sprigs, to garnish

TARTARE SAUCE:
1 egg yolk
1 tsp Dijon mustard
2 tsp white wine vinegar
150 ml/5 fl oz/⅔ cup light olive oil
1 tsp finely chopped green olives
1 tsp finely chopped gherkins
1 tsp finely chopped capers
2 tsp chopped fresh chives
2 tsp chopped fresh parsley
salt and pepper

1 Put the foccacia into the bowl of a food processor and blend to fine crumbs. Set aside. Thinly slice the haddock fillet widthways into fingers. Put the flour, egg and breadcrumbs into separate bowls.

2 Dip the haddock fingers into the flour, then the egg and finally the breadcrumbs to coat. Lay on a plate and refrigerate for 30 minutes. For the tartare sauce, put the egg yolk, mustard, vinegar and seasoning into the bowl of a clean food processor. Blend for 30 seconds until frothy. Begin adding the olive oil, drop by drop, until the mixture begins to thicken. Continue adding the olive oil in a slow, steady stream until all the oil is incorporated.

3 Scrape from the food processor bowl into a small mixing bowl and stir in the olives, gherkins, capers, chives and parsley. Check for seasoning. Add a little hot water if the sauce is too thick.

4 Heat a large pan half filled with vegetable oil to 190°C/375°F or until a cube of bread browns in 30 seconds. Cook the haddock goujons, in batches of 3 or 4 for 3–4 minutes until the crumbs are browned and crisp and the fish is cooked. Drain on the kitchen paper and keep warm while you cook the remaining fish.

5 Serve the haddock goujons immediately, with the tartare sauce and lemon wedges.

1

2

4

Swordfish Steaks

Salsa verde is a classic Italian sauce of herbs, garlic and anchovies. It simply means 'green sauce'.

Serves 4

INGREDIENTS

4 x swordfish steaks, about 150 g/ 5½ oz each
4 tbsp olive oil
1 garlic clove, crushed
1 tsp lemon rind
lemon wedges, to garnish

SALSA VERDE:
25 /1 oz/1 cup flat-leaf parsley leaves
15 g/½ oz/½ cup mixed herbs, such as basil, mint, chives
1 garlic clove, chopped
1 tbsp capers, drained and rinsed
1 tbsp green peppercorns in brine, drained
4 anchovies in oil, drained and roughly chopped
1 tsp Dijon mustard
120 ml/4 fl oz/½ cup extra-virgin olive oil
salt and pepper

1 Wash the dry the swordfish steaks and arrange in a non-metallic dish. Mix together the olive oil, garlic and lemon rind. Pour over the swordfish steaks and leave to marinate for 2 hours.

2 For the salsa verde, put the parsley leaves, mixed herbs, garlic, capers, green peppercorns, anchovies, mustard and olive oil into a food processor or blender. Blend to a smooth paste, adding a little warm water if necessary. Season to taste and set aside.

3 Remove the swordfish steaks from the marinade. Cook on a barbecue or preheated ridged grill pan for 2–3 minutes each side until tender. Serve immediately with the salsa verde and lemon wedges.

VARIATIONS

Any firm fleshed-fish will do this recipe. Try tuna or even shark instead.

Swordfish or Tuna Fajitas

Fajitas are usually made with chicken or lamb but using a firm fish like swordfish or tuna works very well.

Serves 4

INGREDIENTS

3 tbsp olive oil
2 tsp chilli powder
1 tsp ground cumin
pinch cayenne pepper
1 garlic clove, crushed
900 g/2 lb swordfish or tuna
1 red (bell) pepper, deseeded and thinly sliced
1 yellow (bell) pepper, deseeded and thinly sliced
2 courgettes (zucchini), cut into batons
1 large onion, thinly sliced
12 soft flour tortillas
1 tbsp lemon juice
3 tbsp chopped fresh coriander
salt and pepper
150 ml/5 fl oz/⅔ cup soured cream, to serve

GUACAMOLE:
1 large avocado
1 tomato, skinned, deseeded and diced
1 garlic clove, crushed
dash Tabasco
2 tbsp lemon juice
salt and pepper

1 Mix together the oil, chilli powder, cumin, cayenne and garlic. Cut the swordfish or tuna into chunks and mix with the marinade. Set aside for 1–2 hours.

2 Heat a large frying pan (skillet) until hot. Add the fish and its marinade to the pan and cook for 2 minutes, stirring occasionally, until the fish begins to brown. Add the red (bell) pepper, yellow (bell) pepper, courgettes (zucchini) and onion and continue cooking for a further 5 minutes until the vegetables have softened but still firm.

3 Meanwhile, warm the tortillas in a low oven or microwave according to the packet instructions.

4 To make the guacamole, mash the avocado until fairly smooth, stir in the tomato, garlic, Tabasco, lemon juice and seasoning.

5 Add the lemon juice, coriander and seasoning to the vegetable mix. Spoon some of the mixture down the warmed tortilla. Top with guacamole and a spoonful of soured cream and roll up.

Smoked Fish Pie

What fish cook book would be complete without a fish pie? This is a classic version with smoked fish, prawns (shrimp) and vegetables, in a cheesy sauce, with a more unusual grated potato topping.

Serves 6

INGREDIENTS

- 2 tbsp olive oil
- 1 onion, finely chopped
- 1 leek, thinly sliced
- 1 carrot, diced
- 1 celery stick, diced
- 115 g/4 oz/½ cup button mushrooms, halved if large
- grated rind 1 lemon
- 375 g/12 oz skinless, boneless smoked cod or haddock fillet, cubed
- 375 g/12 oz skinless, boneless white fish such as haddock, hake or monkfish, cubed
- 225 g/8 oz cooked peeled prawns (shrimp)
- 2 tbsp chopped fresh parsley
- 1 tbsp chopped fresh dill

SAUCE:

- 50 g/1¾ oz/2 tbsp butter
- 40 g/1½ oz/⅓ cup plain (all-purpose) flour
- 1 tsp mustard powder
- 600 ml/1 pint/2½ cups milk
- 80 g/3 oz/½ cup Gruyère cheese, grated

TOPPING:

- 750 g/1½ lb potatoes, unpeeled
- 50 g/1¾ oz/¼ cup butter, melted
- 25 g/1 oz Gruyère cheese, grated
- salt and pepper

1 For the sauce, heat the butter in a large saucepan and when melted, add the flour and mustard powder. Stir until smooth and cook over a very low heat for 2 minutes without colouring. Slowly beat in the milk until smooth. Simmer gently for 2 minutes then stir in the cheese until smooth. Remove from the heat and put some cling film (plastic wrap) over the surface of the sauce to prevent a skin forming. Set aside.

2 Meanwhile, for the topping, boil the whole potatoes in plenty of salted water for 15 minutes. Drain well and set aside until cool enough to handle.

3 Heat the olive oil in a clean pan and add the onion. Cook for 5 minutes until softened. Add the leek, carrot, celery and mushrooms and cook a further 10 minutes until the vegetables have softened. Stir in the lemon rind and cook briefly.

4 Add the softened vegetables with the fish, prawns (shrimp), parsley and dill to the sauce. Season with salt and pepper and transfer to a greased 1.75 litre/3 pint/7½ cup baking dish.

5 Peel the cooled potatoes and grate coarsely. Mix with the melted butter. Cover the filling with the grated potato and sprinkle with the grated Gruyère cheese.

6 Cover loosely with foil and bake in a preheated oven at 200°C/400°F/Gas Mark 6, for 30 minutes. Remove the foil and bake a further 30 minutes until the topping is tender and golden and the filling is bubbling. Serve immediately with your favourite selection of vegetables.

Hake Steaks with Chermoula

The cooking time may seem long and indeed you could decrease it slightly if you prefer, but in Morocco they like their fish well cooked!

Serves 4

INGREDIENTS

4 hake steaks, about 225 g/8 oz each
115 g/4 oz/1/2 cup pitted green olives

MARINADE:
6 tbsp finely chopped fresh coriander
6 tbsp finely chopped fresh parsley
6 garlic cloves, crushed
1 tbsp ground cumin
1 tsp ground coriander
1 tbsp paprika
pinch cayenne pepper
150 ml/5 fl oz/2/3 cup fresh lemon juice
300 ml/1/2 pint/1 1/4 cups olive oil

1 For the marinade, mix together the coriander, parsley, garlic, cumin, coriander, paprika, cayenne, lemon juice and olive oil.

2 Wash and dry the hake steaks and place in an ovenproof dish. Pour the marinade over the fish and leave for at least 1 hour and preferably overnight.

3 Before cooking, scatter the olives over the fish. Cover the dish with foil.

4 Cook in a preheated oven at 160°C/325°F/Gas Mark 3. Cook for 35–40 minutes until the fish is tender. Serve with freshly cooked vegetables.

VARIATION

Remove the fish from the marinade and dust with seasoned flour. Fry in oil or clarified butter until golden. Warm through the marinade, but do not boil, and serve as a sauce with lemon slices.

1

3

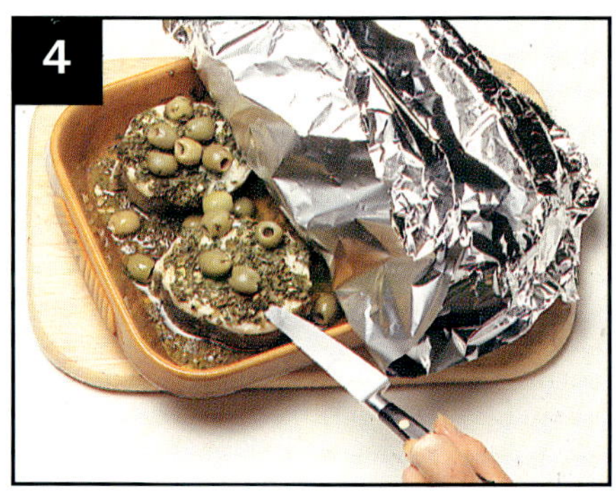

4

Stuffed Mackerel

This is a variation of a Middle Eastern recipe for stuffed mackerel which involves removing the mackerel flesh, while leaving the skin intact, and then re-stuffing the skin. This version is much simpler.

Serves 4

INGREDIENTS

4 large mackerel, cleaned
1 tbsp olive oil
1 small onion, finely sliced
1 tsp ground cinnamon
½ ground ginger
2 tbsp raisins
2 tbsp pine kernels (nuts), toasted
8 vine leaves in brine, drained
salt and pepper

1 Wash and dry the fish and set aside. Heat the oil in a small frying pan (skillet) and add the onion. Cook gently for 5 minutes until softened. Add the cinnamon and ginger and cook for 30 seconds before adding the raisins and pine kernels (nuts). Remove from the heat and allow to cool.

2 Stuff each of the fish with a quarter of the stuffing mixture. Wrap each fish in 2 vine leaves, securing with cocktail sticks (toothpicks).

3 Cook on a preheated barbecue or ridged grill pan for 5 minutes on each side until the vine leaves have scorched and the fish is tender. Serve immediately.

VARIATION

This stuffing works equally well with many other fish, including sea bass and red mullet.

1

2

3

Tuna Fishcakes

This makes a satisfying and quick mid-week supper.

Serves 4

INGREDIENTS

225 g/8 oz potatoes, cubed
1 tbsp olive oil
1 large shallot, finely chopped
1 garlic clove, finely chopped
1 tsp thyme leaves
2 x 200 g/7 oz cans tuna in olive oil, drained
grated rind ½ lemon
1 tbsp chopped fresh parsley
2–3 tbsp plain (all-purpose) flour
1 egg, lightly beaten
115 g/4 oz fresh breadcrumbs
vegetable oil, for shallow frying
salt and pepper

QUICK TOMATO SAUCE:
2 tbsp olive oil
400 g/14 oz can chopped tomatoes
1 garlic clove, crushed
½ tsp sugar
grated rind ½ lemon
1 tbsp chopped fresh basil
salt and pepper

1 For the tuna fishcakes, cook the potatoes in plenty of boiling salted water for 12–15 minutes until tender. Mash, leaving a few lumps, and set aside.

2 Heat the oil in a small frying pan (skillet) and cook the shallot gently for 5 minutes until softened. Add the garlic and thyme leaves and cook for a further minute. Allow to cool slightly then add to the potatoes with the tuna, lemon rind, parsley and seasoning. Mix together well but leave some texture.

3 Form the mixture into 6–8 cakes. Dip the cakes first in the flour, then the egg and finally the breadcrumbs to coat. Refrigerate for 30 minutes.

4 Meanwhile, make the tomato sauce. Put the olive oil, tomatoes, garlic, sugar, lemon rind, basil and seasoning into a saucepan and bring to the boil. Cover and simmer gently for 30 minutes. Uncover and simmer for a further 15 minutes until thickened.

5 Heat enough oil in a frying pan (skillet) to generously cover the bottom. When hot, add the fishcakes in batches and fry for 3–4 minutes each side until golden and crisp. Drain on paper towels while you fry the remaining fishcakes. Serve hot with the tomato sauce.

Sardines with Pesto

This is a very quick and tasty mid-week supper dish. Use a good quality ready-made pesto for an even speedier supper.

Serves 4

INGREDIENTS

- 16 large sardines, scaled and gutted
- 50 g/1¾ oz/2 loosely packed cups fresh basil leaves
- 2 garlic cloves, crushed
- 2 tbsp pine kernels (nuts), toasted
- 50 g/1¾ oz/½ cup freshly grated Parmesan cheese
- 150 ml/5 fl oz/⅔ cup olive oil
- salt and pepper
- lemon wedges, to serve

1 Wash and dry the sardines and arrange on a grill (broiler) pan.

2 Put the basil leaves, garlic and pine kernels (nuts) in a food processor. Blend until finely chopped. Scrape out of the food processor and stir in the Parmesan and oil. Season to taste.

3 Spread a little of the pesto over one side of the sardines and place under a preheated hot grill (broiler) for 3 minutes. Turn the fish, spread with more pesto, and grill (broil) for a further 3 minutes until the sardines are cooked.

4 Serve immediately with extra pesto and lemon wedges.

VARIATION

This treatment will also work well with other small oily fish such as herrings and pilchards.

Salmon Frittata

A frittata is an Italian slow-cooked omelette, not dissimilar from the Spanish tortilla. Here it is filled with poached salmon, fresh herbs and vegetables to make a substantial dish.

Serves 6

INGREDIENTS

250 g/9 oz skinless, boneless salmon
3 sprigs fresh thyme
sprig fresh parsley plus 2 tbsp chopped fresh parsley
5 black peppercorns
½ small onion, sliced
½ stick celery, sliced
½ carrot, chopped
175 g/6 oz asparagus spears, chopped
80 g/3 oz baby carrots, halved
50 g/1¾ oz/¼ cup butter
1 large onion, finely sliced
1 garlic clove, finely chopped
115 g/4 oz/1 cup peas, fresh or frozen
8 eggs, lightly beaten
1 tbsp chopped fresh dill
salt and pepper
lemon wedges, to garnish

TO SERVE:
crème fraîche
salad
crusty bread

1 Place the salmon in a saucepan with 1 sprig of the thyme, the parsley sprig, peppercorns, onion, celery and carrot. Cover the vegetables and fish with cold water and bring slowly to the boil. Remove the saucepan from the heat and leave to stand for 5 minutes. Lift the fish out of the the poaching liquid, flake the flesh and set aside. Discard the poaching liquid.

2 Bring a large saucepan of salted water to the boil and blanch the asparagus for 2 minutes. Drain and refresh under the cold water. Blanch the carrots for 4 minutes. Drain and refresh under cold water. Drain again and pat dry. Set aside.

3 Heat half the butter in a large frying pan (skillet) and add the onion. Cook gently for 8–10 minutes until softened but not coloured. Add the garlic and remaining sprigs of thyme and cook for a further minute. Add the asparagus, carrots and peas and heat through. Remove from the heat.

4 Add the vegetables to the eggs with the chopped parsley, dill, salmon and seasoning and stir briefly. Heat the remaining butter in the pan and return the mixture to the pan. Cover and cook over a low heat for 10 minutes.

5 Cook under a preheated medium grill (broiler) for a further 5 minutes until set and golden. Serve hot or cold in wedges topped with a dollop of crème fraîche, salad and crusty bread. Garnish with lemon wedges.

1

4

Mixed Seafood Brochettes

If your fishmonger sells turbot steaks, you will probably need one large steak for this dish. Remove the skin and bones yourself and chop the flesh into chunks.

Serves 4

INGREDIENTS

225 g/8 oz skinless, boneless turbot fillet
225 g/8 oz skinless, boneless salmon fillet
8 scallops
8 large tiger prawns (jumbo shrimp) or langoustines
16 fresh bay leaves
1 lemon, sliced
4 tbsp olive oil
grated rind 1 lemon
4 tbsp chopped mixed herbs such as thyme, parsley, chives, basil
black pepper

LEMON BUTTER RICE:
175 g/6 oz long-grain rice
grated rind and juice 1 lemon
50 g/1¾ oz/¼ cup butter
salt and pepper

TO GARNISH:
lemon wedges
dill sprigs

1 Chop the turbot and salmon into 8 pieces each. Thread on to 8 skewers, with the scallops and tiger prawns (jumbo shrimp) or langoustines, alternating with the bay leaves and lemon slices. Put into a non-metallic dish in a single layer if possible.

2 Mix together the olive oil, lemon rind, herbs and black pepper. Pour this mixture over the fish. Cover and leave to marinate for 2 hours, turning once or twice

3 For the lemon butter rice, bring a large pan of salted water to the boil and add the rice and lemon rind. Return to the boil and simmer for 7–8 minutes until the rice is tender. Drain well and immediately stir in the lemon juice and butter. Season with salt and pepper to taste.

4 Meanwhile, lift the fish brochettes from their marinade and cook on a lit barbecue or under a preheated hot grill (broiler) for 8–10 minutes, turning regularly, until cooked through. Serve with lemon butter rice. Garnish with lemon wedges and dill.

1

3

4

Char-grilled Scallops

Marinated scallops, char-grilled and served with couscous studded with colourful vegetables and herbs.

Serves 4

INGREDIENTS

16 king scallops
3 tbsp olive oil
grated rind 1 lime
2 tbsp chopped fresh basil
2 tbsp chopped fresh chives
1 garlic clove, finely chopped
black pepper

JEWELLED COUSCOUS:
225 g/ 8 oz couscous
½ yellow (bell) pepper, deseeded and halved
½ red (bell) pepper, deseeded and halved
4 tbsp extra virgin olive oil
115 g/4 oz cucumber, chopped into 1 cm/½ inch pieces
3 spring onions (scallions), finely chopped
1 tbsp lime juice
2 tbsp shredded fresh basil
salt and pepper

TO GARNISH:
basil leaves
lime wedges

1 Clean and trim the scallops as necessary. Put into a non-metallic dish. Mix together the olive oil, lime rind, basil, chives, garlic and black pepper. Pour over the scallops and cover. Leave to marinate for 2 hours.

2 Cook the couscous according to the packet instructions, omitting any butter recommended. Brush the red and yellow (bell) pepper halves with a little of the olive oil and place under a preheated hot grill (broiler) for 5–6 minutes, turning once, until the skins are blackened and the flesh is tender. Put into a plastic bag and leave until cool enough to handle. When cool, peel off the skins and chop the flesh into 1 cm/½ inch pieces. Add to the couscous with the remaining olive oil, cucumber, spring onions (scallions), lemon juice and seasoning. Set aside.

3 Lift the scallops from the marinade and thread on to 4 skewers. Cook on a lit barbecue or preheated ridged grill pan for 1 minute on each side, until charred and firm but not quite cooked through. Remove from the heat and allow to rest for 2 minutes.

4 Stir the shredded basil into the couscous and divide on to plates. Put a skewer on each, garnish with basil leaves and lime wedges.

1

2

3

Prawn (Shrimp) Rostis

These crisp little vegetable and prawn (shrimp) cakes make an ideal light lunch or supper, accompanied with a salad.

Serves 4

INGREDIENTS

- 350 g/12 oz potatoes
- 350 g/12 oz celeriac (celery root)
- 1 carrot
- ½ small onion
- 225 g/8 oz cooked peeled prawns (shrimp), thawed if frozen and well-drained on paper towels
- 25 g/1 oz/¼ cup plain (all-purpose) flour
- 1 egg, lightly beaten
- vegetable oil, for frying
- salt and pepper

CHERRY TOMATO SALSA:

- 225 g/8 oz mixed cherry tomatoes such as baby plum, yellow, orange, pear, quartered
- ½ small mango, finely diced
- 1 red chilli, deseeded and finely chopped
- ½ small red onion, finely chopped
- 1 tbsp chopped fresh coriander
- 1 tbsp chopped fresh chives
- 2 tbsp olive oil
- 2 tsp lemon juice
- salt and pepper

1 For the salsa, mix together the tomatoes, mango, chilli, red onion, coriander, chives, olive oil, lemon juice and seasoning. Set aside for the flavours to infuse.

2 Using a food processor or the fine blade of a box grater, finely grate the potatoes, celeriac (celery root), carrot and onion. Mix together with the prawns (shrimp), flour and egg. Season well and set aside.

3 Divide the prawn (shrimp) mixture into 8 equal pieces. Press each into a greased 10 cm/4 inch cutter (if you only have 1 cutter, simply shape the rostis individually).

4 In a large frying pan (skillet), heat a shallow layer of prawn (shrimp) oil. When hot, transfer the vegetable cakes, still in the cutters, to the frying pan (skillet), in batches if necessary. When the oil sizzles underneath, remove the cutter. Fry gently, pressing down with a spatula, for 6–8 minutes on each side, until crisp and browned and the vegetables are tender. Drain on paper towels. Serve immediately while still hot with the tomato salsa.

1

2

4

Moules Marinières

This dish is much revered in both Belgium and France. Try the chips with a little homemade mayonnaise (see Cod and Chips page 128) and enjoy a truly Belgian feast.

Serves 4

INGREDIENTS

900 g/2 lb live mussels
2 shallots, finely chopped
2 garlic cloves, finely chopped
150 ml/5 fl oz/⅔ cup dry white wine
2 tbsp chopped fresh parsley
salt and pepper

CHIPS:
900 g/2 lb potatoes
vegetable oil, for deep-frying
salt

TO SERVE (OPTIONAL):
lemon wedges
mayonnaise

1 Clean the mussels by scrubbing or scraping the shells and pulling out any beards. Discard any mussels with broken shells or that refuse to close when tapped sharply.

2 For the chips, cut the potatoes into thin strips, about 1 cm/½ inch thick. Fill a large saucepan or chip pan about one third full of vegetable oil and heat to 140°C/275°F or until a cube of bread browns in 1 minute. Add the chips in 3 batches and cook for 5–6 minutes until the chips are tender but not browned. Drain on paper towels.

3 Put the mussels in a large saucepan with the shallots, garlic and white wine. Cook, covered, over a high heat for 3–4 minutes until all the mussels have opened. Discard any mussels that remain closed. Add the parsley and taste for seasoning. Keep warm while you finish the chips.

4 Increase the temperature of the oil to 190°C/375°F, or until a cube of bread browns in 30 seconds. Cook the chips, again in 3 batches, for 2–3 minutes until golden and crisp. Drain on paper towels and sprinkle with salt.

5 Divide the mussels between 4 large serving bowls. Divide the chips between smaller bowls or plates and serve with lemon wedges and plenty of mayonnaise for dipping chips, if liked.

1

2

3

Provençal Mussels

This recipe conjures up southern France – tomatoes, wine, herbs and garlic combine to make a flavourful mussel stew.

Serves 4

INGREDIENTS

- 900 g/2 lb live mussels
- 3 tbsp olive oil
- 1 onion, finely chopped
- 3 garlic cloves, finely chopped
- 2 tsp fresh thyme leaves
- 150 ml/ 5 fl oz/$^{2}/_{3}$ cup red wine
- 2 x 400 g/14 oz cans chopped tomatoes
- 2 tbsp chopped fresh parsley
- salt and pepper
- crusty bread, to serve

1 Clean the mussels by scrubbing or scraping the shells and pulling out any beards. Discard any mussels with broken shells or that do not close when tapped sharply. Put the mussels in a large saucepan with just the water that clings to their shells. Cook, covered, over a high heat for 3–4 minutes until all the mussels have opened. Discard any mussels that remain closed. Drain, reserving the cooking liquid. Set aside.

2 Heat the oil in a large saucepan and add the onion. Cook gently for 8–10 minutes until softened, but not coloured. Add the garlic and thyme and cook for a further 1 minute. Add the red wine and simmer rapidly until reduced and syrupy. Add the tomatoes and strained, reserved mussel cooking liquid and bring to the boil. Cover and simmer for 30 minutes. Uncover and cook for a further 15 minutes.

3 Add the mussels and cook for a further 5 minutes until heated through. Stir in the parsley, season to taste and serve with plenty of fresh crusty bread.

VARIATION

Replace the mussels with an equal quantity of clams.

Pasta, Rice & other Grains

Nutritionists today recommend a diet high in complex carbohydrates, which include pasta, rice, potatoes, breads and grains. A diet based around this food group ensures high energy levels without any dips in blood sugar levels, which can lead to bingeing.

This chapter includes a variety of dishes based on these foods. The most popular of these has to be pasta and there are a number of pasta dishes here. There are also a variety of skill levels catered for, from very simple pasta dishes, like Spaghettini with Crab and Linguini with Sardines, to more complicated dishes, like homemade Squid Ink Pasta, Fideua and Seafood Lasagne.

There are also pies and pasties, such as Herring and Potato Pie and Fish Pasties, as well as rice dishes, including Jambalaya, Lobster Risotto and Prawn & Asparagus Risotto.

Dishes using other grains include Buckwheat Pancakes with Smoked Salmon & Crème Fraîche, Fish & Bread Soup and Pizza Marinara.

Tagliatelle with Broccoli & Anchovies

This is based on a Sicilian dish combining broccoli and anchovies, but I have added lemon and garlic for more flavour.

Serves 4

INGREDIENTS

6 tbsp olive oil
50 g/1¾ oz fresh white breadcrumbs
450g/1 lb broccoli, cut into small florets
350 g/12 oz dried tagliatelle
4 anchovy fillets, drained and chopped
2 garlic cloves, sliced
grated rind 1 lemon
large pinch chilli flakes
salt and pepper
freshly grated Parmesan cheese, to serve

1 Heat 2 tablespoons of the olive oil in a frying pan (skillet) and add the breadcrumbs. Stir-fry over a medium heat for 4–5 minutes until golden and crisp. Drain on paper towels.

2 Bring a large pan of salted water to the boil and add the broccoli. Blanch for 3 minutes then drain, reserving the water. Refresh the broccoli under cold water and drain again. Pat dry on paper towels and set. Set aside.

3 Bring the water back to the boil and add the tagliatelle. Cook according to the packet instructions until tender but still firm to the bite.

4 Meanwhile, heat another 2 tablespoons of the oil in a l arge frying pan (skillet) or wok and add the anchovies. Cook for minute then mash with a wooden spoon to a paste. Add the garlic, lemon rind and chilli flakes and cook gently for 2 minutes. Add the broccoli and cook for a further 3–4 minutes until hot.

5 Drain the cooked pasta and add to the broccoli mixture with the remaining 2 tbsp olive oil and seasoning. Toss together well.

6 Divide the tagliatelle between serving plates. Top with the fried breadcrumbs and Parmesan cheese and serve immediately.

Pasta Puttanesca

The story goes that this is a sauce made and eaten by Italian prostitutes who needed a quick and simple meal to keep them going. Most of the ingredients you will have in the store cupboard.

Serves 4

INGREDIENTS

3 tbsp extra-virgin olive oil
1 large red onion, finely chopped
4 anchovy fillets, drained
pinch chilli flakes
2 garlic cloves, finely chopped
400 g/14 oz can chopped tomatoes
2 tbsp tomato purée (paste)
225 g/8 oz dried spaghetti
25 g/1 oz pitted black olives, roughly chopped
25 g/1 oz pitted green olives, roughly chopped
1 tbsp capers, drained and rinsed
4 sun-dried tomatoes, roughly chopped
salt and pepper

1 Heat the oil in a saucepan and add the onion, anchovies and chilli flakes. Cook for 10 minutes until softened and starting to brown. Add the garlic and cook for 30 seconds.

2 Add the tomatoes and tomato purée (paste) and bring to the boil. Simmer gently for 10 minutes.

3 Meanwhile, cook the spaghetti in plenty of boiling salted water according to the packet instructions until tender but still firm to the bite.

4 Add the olives, capers and sun-dried tomatoes to the sauce. Simmer for a further 2–3 minutes. Season to taste.

5 Drain the pasta well and stir in the sauce. Toss well to mix. Serve immediately.

Seafood Lasagne

A rich dish of layers of pasta, with seafood and mushrooms in a tomato sauce, topped with béchamel sauce and baked until golden.

Serves 6

INGREDIENTS

- 50 g/1¾ oz/¼ cup butter
- 40 g/1½ oz/6 tbsp flour
- 1 tsp mustard powder
- 600 ml/1 pint/2½ cups milk
- 2 tbsp olive oil
- 1 onion, chopped
- 2 garlic cloves, finely chopped
- 1 tbsp fresh thyme leaves
- 450 g/1 lb/3 cups mixed mushrooms, sliced
- 150 ml/5 fl oz/⅔ cup white wine
- 400 g/14 oz can chopped tomatoes
- 450 g/1 lb mixed skinless white fish fillets, cubed
- 225 g/8 oz fresh scallops, trimmed
- 4–6 sheets fresh lasagne
- 225 g/8 oz Mozzarella, drained and chopped
- salt and pepper

1 Melt the butter in a saucepan. Add the flour and mustard powder and stir until smooth. Simmer gently for 2 minutes without colouring. Gradually add the milk, whisking until smooth. Bring to the boil and simmer for 2 minutes. Remove from the heat and set aside. Cover the surface of the sauce with cling film (plastic wrap) to prevent a skin forming.

2 Heat the oil in a frying pan (skillet) and add the onion, garlic and thyme. Cook gently for 5 minutes until softened. Add the mushrooms and fry for a further 5 minutes until softened. Stir in the wine and boil rapidly until nearly evaporated. Stir in the tomatoes. Bring to the boil and simmer, covered, for 15 minutes. Season and set aside.

3 Lightly grease a lasagne dish. Spoon half the tomato sauce over the base of the dish and top with half the fish and scallops.

4 Layer half the lasagne over the fish, pour over half the white sauce, add half the Mozzarella. Repeat these layers, finishing with the white sauce and Mozzarella.

5 Bake in a preheated oven at 200°C/400°F/Gas Mark 6 for 35–40 minutes until bubbling and golden and the fish is cooked through. Remove from the oven and leave to stand on a heat resistant surface or mat for 10 minutes before serving.

2

3

4

Spaghetti al Vongole

This is a very full-flavoured and elegant looking dish, especially if you can find small clams which often have richly coloured shells.

Serves 4

INGREDIENTS

- 900 g/2 lb live clams, scrubbed
- 2 tbsp olive oil
- 1 large onion, finely chopped
- 2 garlic cloves, finely chopped
- 1 tsp fresh thyme leaves
- 150 ml/5 fl oz/$^{2}/_{3}$ cup white wine
- 400 g/14 oz can chopped tomatoes
- 350 g/12 oz dried spaghetti
- 1 tbsp chopped fresh parsley
- salt and pepper

1 Put the clams into a large saucepan with just the water clinging to their shells. Cook, covered, over a high heat for 3–4 minutes, shaking the pan occasionally, until all the clams have opened. Remove from the heat and strain, reserving the cooking liquid. Discard any clams that remain closed. Set aside.

2 Heat the oil in a saucepan and add the onion. Cook for 10 minutes over a low heat until softened but not coloured. Add the garlic and thyme and cook for a further 30 seconds. Increase the heat and add the white wine. Simmer rapidly until reduced and syrupy. Add the tomatoes and reserved clam cooking liquid. Cover and simmer for 15 minutes. Uncover and simmer for a further 15 minutes until thickened. Season to taste.

3 Meanwhile, cook the spaghetti in plenty of boiling salted water according to the packet instructions, until tender but still firm to the bite. Drain well and return to the pan.

4 Add the clams to the tomato sauce and heat through for 2–3 minutes. Add the parsley and stir well. Add the tomato sauce to the pasta and toss together until the pasta is well coated in sauce. Serve immediately.

COOK'S TIP

If you are only able to get very large clams, reserve a few in their shells to garnish and shell the rest.

Linguini with Sardines

This is a very quick dish that is ideal for mid-week suppers as it is so simple to prepare but full of flavour.

Serves 4

INGREDIENTS

8 sardines, filleted
1 bulb fennel
4 tbsp olive oil
3 garlic cloves, sliced
1 tsp chilli flakes
350 g/12 oz dried linguine
½ tsp finely grated lemon rind
1 tbsp lemon juice
2 tbsp pine kernels (nuts), toasted
2 tbsp chopped fresh parsley
salt and pepper

1 Wash and dry the sardine fillets. Roughly chop into large pieces and set aside. Trim the fennel bulb and slice very thinly.

2 Heat 2 tabelspoons of the olive oil in a large frying pan (skillet) and add the garlic and chilli flakes. Cook for 1 minute then add the fennel. Cook over a medium high heat for 4–5 minutes until softened. Add the sardine pieces and cook for a further 3–4 minutes until just cooked.

3 Meanwhile, cook the pasta in plenty of boiling salted water according to the packet instructions, until tender but still firm to the bite. Drain well and return to the pan.

4 Add the lemon rind, lemon juice, pine kernels (nuts), parsley and seasonings to the sardines and toss together. Add to the pasta with the remaining olive oil and toss together gently. Serve immediately while the pasta is still hot with a sprinkling of parsley.

COOK'S TIP

Reserve a couple of tablespoons of the pasta cooking water and add to the pasta with the sauce if the mixture seems a little dry.

Crab Ravioli

Although it is time-consuming to make and fill your own pasta, the flavour and texture are unbeatable.

Serves 4

INGREDIENTS

225 g/8 oz/2 cups strong white bread flour, or type '00' Italian pasta flour
1 tsp salt
2 eggs plus 1 egg yolk
1 tbsp olive oil
225 g/8 oz raw prawns (shrimp), finely chopped
225 g/8 oz white crab meat
1 tbsp chopped fresh chervil
1 tbsp chopped fresh chives
1 tbsp chopped fresh parsley
1 tsp grated rind lime
4 tbsp double (heavy) cream
salt and pepper

RED (BELL) PEPPER SAUCE:
½ large red (bell) pepper, cored, deseeded and halved
1 tsp olive oil, for brushing
50 g/1¾ oz/¼ cup unsalted butter, softened
1 tbsp lime juice
salt and pepper

TO GARNISH:
lime wedges
fresh chives

1 To make the pepper sauce, brush the pepper pieces with the olive oil. Place under a preheated hot grill (broiler) for 3–4 minutes on each side until charred and tender. Remove from the heat and place in a plastic bag until cool enough to handle. Discard the skin and put in a food processor or blender. Add the butter, lime juice and seasoning and blend until smooth. Set aside.

2 To make the pasta, sift the flour and salt into a bowl. Make a well in the centre and add the eggs, egg yolk, oil and enough water to make a firm dough. Knead for 5 minutes. Wrap in cling film (plastic wrap) and chill.

3 Meanwhile, mix together the prawns (shrimp), crab, chervil, chives, parsley, lime rind, cream and seasoning and set aside.

4 Divide the pasta dough into 8 pieces. Using a pasta machine, roll out each piece as thinly as possible. Dust the surface liberally with flour and top with 1 sheet of pasta. Place a teaspoon of filling at 2.5 cm/1 inch intervals along the dough. Brush lightly around the filling with water then place a second sheet of pasta on top.

5 Press down firmly around each mound of filling to seal then, using a pastry cutter or pasta wheel, cut out the ravioli. Repeat with the remaining pasta and filling, placing the cut out ravioli on a well-floured tea towel (dish cloth).

6 Bring a large saucepan of lightly salted water to the boil and add the ravioli. Boil for 3–4 minutes until the pasta is tender but still firm to the bite. Drain well and toss immediately with the pepper sauce. Serve immediately, while the ravioli is still hot garnished with lime wedges and snipped fresh chives.

Spaghettini with Crab

This dish is probably one of the simplest in the book, yet the flavour is as impressive as a recipe over which you have slaved for hours.

Serves 4

INGREDIENTS

1 dressed crab, about 450 g/1 lb including the shell
350 g/12 oz dried spaghettini
6 tbsp best quality extra-virgin olive oil
1 hot red chilli, deseeded and finely chopped
2 garlic cloves, finely chopped
3 tbsp chopped fresh parsley
1 tsp finely grated lemon juice
2 tbsp lemon juice
salt and pepper
lemon wedges, to garnish

1 Scoop the meat from the crab shell into a bowl. Mix the white and brown meat lightly together and set aside.

2 Bring a large saucepan of salted water to the boil and add the spaghettini. Cook according to the instructions on the packet until tender but still firm to the bite. Drain well and return to the pan.

3 Meanwhile, heat 2 tablespoons of the olive oil in a frying pan (skillet). When hot, add the chilli and garlic. Cook for 30 seconds before adding the crab meat, parsley, lemon juice and lemon rind. Stir-fry for a further minute until the crab is just heated through.

4 Add the crab mixture to the pasta with the remaining olive oil and seasoning. Toss together thoroughly and serve immediately, garnished with lemon wedges.

COOK'S TIP

If you prefer to buy your own fresh crab you will need a large crab weighing about 1 kg/2 lb 4 oz.

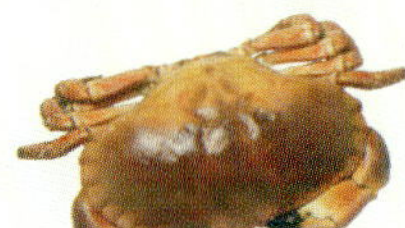

Squid Ink Pasta

This is a dramatic looking dish, with its jet-black pasta and rich sauce of squid. Definitely one for special occasions.

Serves 6

INGREDIENTS

450 g/1 lb squid with their ink
300 g/10½ oz 2½ cups strong white bread flour or Italian type '00' flour
100 g/3½ oz fine semolina
2 eggs

SAUCE:
4 tbsp olive oil
2 garlic cloves, finely chopped
1 tsp paprika
3 plum tomatoes, peeled, deseeded and diced
150 ml/5 fl oz/⅔ cup white wine
1 tbsp chopped fresh parsley
salt and pepper

1 To prepare the squid and its ink, carefully grasp the head and tentacles of the squid and pull to remove all the innards. The ink sac lies at the furthest point from the tentacles and is a silverish tube – be careful to keep it intact. Cut the ink sac away from the innards and set aside. Cut the tentacles just below the beak and discard the remaining innards. Remove the stiff cartilage from the body and remove the wings and skin. Wash the body and tentacles well.

2 Slice the body widthways into rings and set aside with the tentacles. Slit open the ink sac and dilute with water to make 50 ml/2 fl oz/¼ cup. Set aside.

3 To make the pasta, sift together the flour and semolina. Make a well in the centre and add the eggs. Using a wooden spoon, draw the flour and eggs together. Gradually add the squid ink – you may not need it all. Mix to a firm dough. Add a little more water if it seems too stiff and a little more flour if it seems too wet. Alternatively, put all the ingredients in the bowl of a mixer fitted with a kneading hook and mix together. Knead the dough for 10 minutes until smooth and elastic. The dough should have the feel of soft leather and be neither sticky nor should it break easily. Wrap in clingfilm (plastic wrap) and set aside for 30 minutes.

4 Using a pasta machine, thinly roll out the dough and cut into thin ribbons. Hang to dry.

5 Meanwhile, make the sauce, heat the oil in a saucepan and then add the garlic and paprika. Fry over a medium heat for 30 seconds. Add the squid and, keeping the heat high, cook for 4–5 minutes until lightly browned and firm. Add the tomatoes and cook for 3–4 minutes until collapsed. Add the white wine and simmer gently for 15 minutes. Stir in the parsley and season to taste.

6 Meanwhile, bring a large pan of salted water to the boil and add the pasta. Cook for 2–3 minutes until tender but still firm to the bite then drain thoroughly. Turn into a large serving bowl, toss together with the sauce and serve immediately.

Fideua

Fideua is a pasta dish which can be found south of Valencia, in western Spain. It is very like a paella but is made with very fine pasta instead of rice.

Serves 6

INGREDIENTS

3 tbsp olive oil
1 large onion, chopped
2 garlic cloves, finely chopped
pinch saffron, crushed
½ tsp paprika
3 tomatoes, skinned, deseeded and chopped
350 g/12 oz egg vermicelli, broken roughly into 5 cm/2 inch lengths
150 ml/5 fl oz/⅔ cup white wine
300 ml/ ½ pint/1¼ cups fish stock
12 large raw prawns (jumbo shrimp)
18 live mussels, scrubbed and bearded
350 g/12 oz cleaned squid, cut into rings
18 large clams, scrubbed
2 tbsp chopped fresh parsley
salt and pepper
lemon wedges, to serve

1 Heat the oil in a large frying pan (skillet) or paella pan. Add the onion and cook gently for 5 minutes until softened. Add the garlic and cook for a further 30 seconds. Add the saffron and paprika and stir well. Add the tomatoes and cook for a further 2–3 minutes until they have collapsed.

2 Add the vermicelli and stir well. Add the wine and boil rapidly until absorbed.

3 Add the fish stock, prawns (shrimp), mussels, squid and clams. Stir and return to a low simmer for 10 minutes until the prawns (shrimp) and squid are cooked through and the mussels and clams have opened. The stock should be almost completely absorbed.

4 Add the parsley and season to taste. Serve immediately, in warm bowls, garnished with lemon wedges.

VARIATION

Use whatever combination of seafood you prefer. Try langoustines, prawns (shrimp) and monkfish.

Thai Noodles

The classic Thai noodle dish, is flavoured with fish sauce, roasted peanuts and prawns.

Serves 4

INGREDIENTS

- 350 g/12 oz cooked, peeled tiger prawns (jumbo shrimp)
- 115 g/4 oz flat rice noodles or rice vermicelli
- 4 tbsp vegetable oil
- 2 garlic cloves, finely chopped
- 1 egg
- 2 tbsp lemon juice
- 1½ tbsp Thai fish sauce
- ½ tsp sugar
- 2 tbsp chopped, roasted peanuts
- ½ tsp cayenne pepper
- 2 spring onions (scallions), cut into 2.5 cm/1 inch pieces
- 50 g/1¾ oz fresh bean-sprouts
- 1 tbsp chopped fresh coriander
- lemon wedges, to serve

1 Drain the prawns on paper towels to remove excess moisture. Set aside. Cook the rice noodles according to the packet instructions. Drain well and set aside.

2 Heat the oil in a wok or large frying pan (skillet) and add the garlic. Fry until just golden. Add the egg and stir quickly to break it up. Cook for a few seconds.

3 Add the prawns (shrimp) and noodles, scraping down the sides of the pan to ensure they mix with the egg and garlic.

4 Add the lemon juice, fish sauce, sugar, half the peanuts, cayenne pepper, the spring onions (scallions) and half the bean-sprouts stirring quickly all the time. Cook over a high heat for a further 2 minutes until everything is heated through.

5 Turn on to a serving plate. Top with the remaining peanuts and bean-sprouts and sprinkle with the coriander. Serve with lemon wedges.

VARIATION

This is a basic dish to which lots of different cooked seafood could be added. Cooked squid rings, mussels and langoustines would all work just as well.

Kedgeree

Originally, kedgeree or khichri was a Hindi dish of rice and lentils, varied with fish or meat in all kinds of ways. It has come to be a dish of rice, spices and smoked fish served with hard-boiled (hard-cooked) eggs, often for breakfast.

Serves 4

INGREDIENTS

450 g/1 lb undyed smoked haddock fillet
2 tbsp olive oil
1 large onion, chopped
2 garlic cloves, finely chopped
½ tsp ground turmeric
½ tsp ground cumin
1 tsp ground coriander
175 g/6 oz/¾ cup basmati rice
4 medium eggs
25 g/1 oz/2 tbsp butter
1 tbsp chopped fresh parsley

TO SERVE:
lemon wedges
mango chutney

1 Pour boiling water over the haddock fillet and leave for 10 minutes. Lift the fish from the cooking water, discard the skin and bones and flake the fish. Set aside. Reserve the cooking water.

2 Heat the oil in a large saucepan and add the onion. Cook for 10 minutes over a medium heat until starting to brown. Add the garlic and cook for a further 30 seconds. Add the turmeric, cumin and coriander and stir-fry for 30 seconds until the spices smell fragrant. Add the rice and stir well.

3 Measure 350 ml/12 fl oz/1½ cups of the haddock cooking water and add this to the pan. Stir well and bring to the boil. Cover and cook over a very low heat for 12–15 minutes until the rice is tender and the stock is absorbed.

4 Meanwhile, bring a small saucepan of water to the boil and add the eggs. When the water has returned to the boil cook the eggs for 8 minutes. Immediately drain the eggs and refresh under cold water to stop them cooking. Set aside.

5 Add the reserved fish pieces, the butter and parsley to the rice. Turn on to a large serving dish. Shell and quarter the eggs and arrange on top of the rice. Serve with lemon wedges and mango chutney.

1

2

5

A Modern Kedgeree

This is a modern version of the classic dish, using smoked salmon as well as fresh salmon and lots of fresh herbs. This is suitable for a smart dinner party and would serve 6 as a starter.

Serves 4

INGREDIENTS

- 25 g/1 oz/2 tbsp butter
- 1 tbsp olive oil
- 1 onion, finely chopped
- 1 garlic clove, finely chopped
- 175 g g/6 oz/¾ cup long-grain rice
- 400 ml/14 fl oz/1⅔ cups fish stock
- 175 g/6 oz skinless, boneless salmon fillet, chopped
- 80 g/3 oz smoked salmon, chopped
- 2 tbsp double (heavy) cream
- 2 tbsp chopped fresh dill
- 3 spring onions (scallions), finely chopped
- salt and pepper
- lemon slices and fresh dill, to garnish

1 Melt the butter with the oil in a large saucepan. Add the onion and cook gently for 10 minutes until softened but not coloured. Add the garlic and cook for a further 30 seconds.

2 Add the rice and cook for 2–3 minutes, stirring, until transparent. Add the fish stock and stir well. Bring to the boil, cover and simmer very gently for 10 minutes.

3 Add the salmon fillet and the smoked salmon and stir well, adding a little more stock or water if it seems dry. Return to the heat and cook a further 6–8 minutes until the fish and rice are tender and all the stock is absorbed.

4 Remove from the heat – or make sure that your gas ring is turned off – and stir in the cream, dill and spring onions (scallions). Season to taste and serve immediately, garnished with a sprig of dill and slice of lemon.

COOK'S TIP

Use smoked salmon trimmings for a budget dish.

2

3

4

Jambalaya

Jambalaya is a dish of Cajun origin. There are as many versions of this dish as there are people who cook it. Here is a straightforward one, using prawns (shrimp), chicken and smoked sausage.

Serves 4

INGREDIENTS

- 2 tbsp vegetable oil
- 2 onions, roughly chopped
- 1 green (bell) pepper, deseeded and roughly chopped
- 2 celery sticks, roughly chopped
- 3 garlic cloves, finely chopped
- 2 tsp paprika
- 300 g/10½ oz skinless, boneless chicken breasts, chopped
- 100 g/3½ oz kabanos sausages, chopped
- 3 tomatoes, skinned and chopped
- 450 g/1 lb/2 cups long-grain rice
- 900 ml/1½ pint/3¾ cups hot chicken or fish stock
- 1 tsp dried oregano
- 2 fresh bay leaves
- 12 large prawn tails (jumbo shrimp tails)
- 4 spring onions (scallions), finely chopped
- 2 tbsp chopped fresh parsley
- salt and pepper
- salad, to serve

1 Heat the vegetable oil in a large frying pan (skillet) and add the onions, (bell) pepper, celery and garlic. Cook for 8–10 minutes until all the vegetables have softened. Add the paprika and cook for a further 30 seconds. Add the chicken and sausages and cook for 8–10 minutes until lightly browned. Add the tomatoes and cook for 2–3 minutes until collapsed.

2 Add the rice to the pan and stir well. Pour in the hot stock, oregano and bay leaves and stir well. Cover and simmer for 10 minutes over a very low heat.

3 Add the prawns (shrimp) and stir well. Cover again and cook for a further 6–8 minutes until the rice is tender and the prawns (shrimp) are cooked through.

4 Stir in the spring onions (scallions), parsley and season to taste. Serve immediately.

COOK'S TIP

Jambalaya is a dish which has some basic ingredients – onions, green (bell) peppers, celery, rice and seasonings – to which you can add whatever you have to hand.

1

2

3

Lobster Risotto

This is a special occasion dish, just for two. You could easily double the recipe for a dinner party.

Serves 2

INGREDIENTS

1 cooked lobster, about 400–450 g/14 oz–1 lb
50 g/1¾ oz/¼ cup butter
1 tbsp olive oil
1 onion, finely chopped
1 garlic clove, finely chopped
1 tsp fresh thyme leaves
175 g/6 oz/¾ cup arborio rice
600 ml/1 pint/2½ cups hot fish stock
150 ml/5 fl oz/⅔ cup sparkling wine
1 tsp green or pink peppercorns in brine, drained and roughly chopped
1 tbsp chopped fresh parsley

1 To prepare the lobster, remove the claws by twisting. Crack the claws using the back of a large knife and set aside. Split the body lengthways. Remove and discard the intestinal vein which runs down the tail, the stomach sac and the spongy looking gills. Remove the meat from the tail and roughly chop. Set aside with the claws.

2 Heat half the butter and the oil in a large frying pan (skillet). Add the onion and cook gently for 4–5 minutes until softened. Add the garlic and cook for a further 30 seconds. Add the thyme and the rice. Stir well for 1–2 minutes, until the rice is well coated in the butter and oil and begins to look translucent.

3 Keep the stock on a low heat. Increase the heat under the frying pan (skillet) to medium and begin adding the stock, a ladleful at a time, stirring well between additions. Continue until all the stock has been absorbed. This should take 20–25 minutes.

4 Add the lobster meat and claws. Stir in the sparkling wine, increasing the heat. When the wine is absorbed, remove the pan from the heat and stir in the green or pink peppercorns, remaining butter and parsley. Leave to stand for 1 minute then serve immediately.

VARIATION

For a slightly cheaper version substitute 450 g/1 lb prawns (shrimp) for the lobster.

Prawn & Asparagus Risotto

An unusual and striking dish with fresh prawns (shrimp) and asparagus is very simple to prepare and ideal for impromptu supper parties.

Serves 4

INGREDIENTS

- 1.2 litres/2 pints/5 cups vegetable stock
- 375 g/12 oz asparagus, cut into 5 cm/2 inch lengths
- 2 tbsp olive oil
- 1 onion, finely chopped
- 1 garlic clove, finely chopped
- 375 g/12 oz/1½ cups arborio rice
- 450 g/1 lb raw tiger prawns (jumbo shrimp), peeled and de-veined
- 2 tbsp olive paste or tapenade
- 2 tbsp chopped fresh basil
- salt and pepper
- Parmesan cheese, to garnish

1 Bring the vegetable stock to the boil in a large saucepan. Add the asparagus and cook for 3 minutes until just tender. Strain, reserving the stock, and refresh the asparagus under cold running water. Drain and set aside.

2 Heat the oil in a large frying pan (skillet), add the onion and cook gently for 5 minutes until softened. Add the garlic and cook for a further 30 seconds. Add the rice and stir for 1–2 minutes until coated with the oil and slightly translucent.

3 Keep the stock on a low heat. Increase the heat under the frying pan (skillet) to medium and begin adding the stock, a ladleful at a time, stirring well between additions. Continue until almost all the stock has been absorbed. This should take 20–25 minutes.

4 Add the prawns (shrimp) and asparagus with the last ladleful of stock and cook for a further 5 minutes until the prawns (shrimp) and rice are tender and the stock has been absorbed. Remove from the heat.

5 Stir in the olive paste, basil and seasoning and leave to stand for 1 minute. Serve immediately, garnished with Parmesan shavings.

1

3

4

Spicy Coconut Rice with Monkfish & Peas

A Thai-influenced dish of rice, cooked in coconut milk, with spicy grilled monkfish and fresh peas.

Serves 4

INGREDIENTS

- 1 hot red chilli, deseeded and chopped
- 1 tsp crushed chilli flakes
- 2 garlic cloves, chopped
- 2 pinches saffron
- 3 tbsp roughly chopped mint leaves
- 4 tbsp olive oil
- 2 tbsp lemon juice
- 375 g/12 oz monkfish fillet, cut into bite-sized pieces
- 1 onion, finely chopped
- 225 g/8 oz long grain rice
- 400g/14 oz can chopped tomatoes
- 200 ml/7 fl oz/¾ cup coconut milk
- 115 g/4 oz peas
- salt and pepper
- 2 tbsp chopped fresh coriander, to garnish

1 In a food processor or blender, blend together the fresh and dried chilli, garlic, saffron, mint, olive oil and lemon juice until finely chopped but not smooth.

2 Put the monkfish into a non-metallic dish and pour over the spice paste, mixing together well. Set aside for 20 minutes to marinate.

3 Heat a large saucepan until very hot. Using a slotted spoon, lift the monkfish from the marinade and add in batches to the hot pan. Cook for 3–4 minutes until browned and firm. Remove with a slotted spoon and set aside.

4 Add the onion and remaining marinade to the same pan and cook for 5 minutes until softened and lightly browned. Add the rice and stir until well coated. Add the tomatoes and coconut milk. Bring to the boil, cover and simmer very gently for 15 minutes. Stir in the peas, season and arrange the fish over the top. Cover with foil and continue to cook over a very low heat for 5 minutes. Serve garnished with the chopped coriander.

Fish & Bread Soup

I haven't specified types of fish for this soup – use whatever is available. Good fish to choose might include eel, skate or cod. Avoid oily fish such as mackerel, herring and salmon.

Serves 6–8

INGREDIENTS

1.75 kg/4 lb mixed whole fish
225 g/8 oz raw prawns (shrimp), shell on
2.25 litres/4 pints/10 cups water
150 ml/5 fl oz/⅔ cup olive oil
2 large onions, roughly chopped
2 celery sticks, roughly chopped
1 leek, roughly chopped
1 small fennel bulb, roughly chopped
5 garlic cloves, chopped
1 strip orange peel
3 tbsp orange juice
400 g/14 oz can chopped tomatoes
1 red (bell) pepper, deseeded and sliced
1 bay leaf
1 sprig fresh thyme
large pinch saffron
large pinch cayenne pepper
6–8 thick slices sourdough bread
salt and pepper

RED (BELL) PEPPER AND SAFFRON SAUCE:
1 red (bell) pepper, deseeded and quartered
1 egg yolk
large pinch saffron
pinch chilli flakes
150 ml/5 fl oz/⅔ cup olive oil
lemon juice, if necessary
salt and pepper

1 Fillet the fish, reserving all the bones. Roughly chop the flesh. Peel the prawns (shrimp). Place the fish bones and the shells in a large saucepan with the water and bring to the boil. Simmer for 20 minutes then strain.

2 Heat the oil in a large pan and add the onions, celery, leek, fennel and garlic. Cook gently for 20 minutes without colouring. Add the orange peel and juice, tomatoes, red (bell) pepper, bay leaf, thyme, saffron, prawns (shrimp) and fish fillets and stock, bring to the boil and simmer for 40 minutes.

3 To prepare the sauce. Brush the red (bell) pepper quarters with some of the olive oil. Place under a hot preheated grill (broiler) for 8–10 minutes, turning once, until the skins have blackened and the flesh is tender. Put in a plastic bag.

4 Once cool, peel off the skin. Roughly chop the flesh and place in a food processor with the egg yolk, saffron, chilli flakes and seasoning. Blend until the red (bell) pepper is smooth. Add the olive oil, in a slow stream, until the sauce begins to thicken. Continue adding in a steady stream. Add seasoning to taste and lemon juice if required.

5 When the soup is cooked, put in a food processor or blender, blend until smooth and push through a sieve with a wooden spoon. Return to the heat and season with cayenne, salt and pepper to taste.

6 Toast the bread on both sides and place in the bottom of soup plates. Ladle over the soup and serve with the sauce.

Herring & Potato Pie

The combination of herrings, apples and potatoes is popular throughout northern Europe. In salads, one often sees the addition of beetroot.

Serves 4

INGREDIENTS

1 tbsp Dijon mustard
115 g/4 oz/½ cup butter, softened
450 g/1 lb herrings, filleted
750 g/1 lb 10 oz potatoes
2 cooking apples, sliced thinly
1 large onion, sliced
1 tsp chopped fresh sage
600 ml/1 pint/2½ cups hot fish stock (to come halfway up the sides of the dish)
50 g/1¾ oz/1 cup crustless ciabatta bread, crumbs
salt and pepper
parsley sprigs, to garnish

1 Mix the mustard with 25 g/1 oz/2 tablespoons of the butter until smooth. Spread this mixture over the cut sides of the herring fillets. Season and roll up the fillets. Set aside. Generously grease a 2 litre/4 pint/8 cup pie dish with some of the remaining butter.

2 Thinly slice the potatoes, using a mandolin if possible. Blanch for 3 minutes in plenty of boiling, salted water until just tender. Drain well, refresh under cold water and pat dry.

3 Heat 25 g/1 oz/2 tablespoons of the remaining butter in a frying pan (skillet) and add the onion. Cook gently for 8–10 minutes until softened but not coloured. Remove from the heat and set aside.

4 Put half the potato slices into the bottom of the pie dish with some seasoning then add half the apple and half the onion. Put the herring fillets on top of the onion and sprinkle with the sage. Repeat the layers in reverse order, ending with potato. Season well and add the hot stock.

5 Melt the remaining butter and stir in the breadcrumbs until well combined. Sprinkle the breadcrumbs over the pie. Bake in a preheated oven, at 190°C/375°F/Gas Mark 5 for 40–50 minutes until the breadcrumbs are golden and the herrings are cooked through. Serve garnished with parsley.

VARIATION

If herrings are unavailable, substitute mackerel or sardines.

Salt Cod Hash

As well as being a simple supper dish, this would make a delicious addition to a brunch menu.

Serves 4

INGREDIENTS

½ quantity Home-salted Cod (see page 90)
4 eggs
3 tbsp olive oil, plus extra for drizzling
8 rashers rindless smoked streaky bacon, chopped
700 g/1 lb 9 oz old potatoes, diced
8 garlic cloves
8 thick slices good-quality white bread
2 plum tomatoes, skinned and chopped
2 tsp red wine vinegar
2 tbsp chopped fresh parsley plus extra to garnish
salt and pepper
lemon wedges, to garnish

1 Soak the prepared cod in cold water for 2 hours. Drain well. Bring a large saucepan of water to the boil and add the fish. Remove from the heat and leave to stand for 10 minutes. Drain the fish on paper towels and flake the flesh. Set aside. Discard the soaking water.

2 Bring a saucepan of water to the boil and add the eggs. Simmer the eggs for 7–9 minutes from when the water returns to the boil – 7 minutes for a slightly soft centre, 9 for a firm centre. Immediately drain then plunge the eggs into cold water to stop them cooking further. When cool enough to handle, shell the eggs and roughly chop. Set aside.

3 Heat the oil in a large frying pan (skillet) and add the bacon. Cook over a medium heat for 4–5 minutes until crisp and brown. Remove with a slotted spoon and drain on paper towel. Add the potatoes to the pan with the garlic and cook over a medium heat for 8–10 minutes until crisp and golden.

4 Toast the bread on both sides until golden. Drizzle with olive oil and set aside.

5 Add the plum tomatoes, bacon, fish, vinegar and reserved chopped egg to the potatoes and garlic. Cook for a further 2 minutes.Stir in the parsley and season to taste. Put the toast plates and topped with hash parsley and lemon wedges.

Pizza Marinara

Traditionally, a pizza topped with mixed seafood would have no cheese but in this case it helps to protect the fish from overcooking as well as adding texture.

Serves 4

INGREDIENTS

225 g/8 oz/2 cups strong white bread flour
1 tsp salt
7 g sachet easy-blend yeast
2 tbsp olive oil
150 ml/5 fl oz/⅔ cup hand-hot water

TOMATO SAUCE:
2 tbsp olive oil
1 small onion, finely chopped
1 garlic clove, crushed
400 g/14 oz can chopped tomatoes
1 tsp dried oregano
1 tbsp tomato purèe (paste)
salt and pepper

MIXED SEAFOOD:
16 live mussels, scrubbed and bearded
16 large clams, scrubbed
1 tbsp olive oil
12 raw tiger prawns (jumbo shrimp)
225 g/8 oz cleaned squid, cut into rings
2 x 150 g/5½ oz balls Mozzarella, drained and sliced
olive oil, for drizzling
handful basil leaves
salt and pepper

1 To make the pizza base, in a large bowl mix together the flour, salt and yeast. Add the oil and enough water to make a soft, firm dough. Knead on a floured surface and knead for 5 minutes until smooth and elastic.

2 Form dough into a neat ball and drop into an oiled bowl. Lightly oil the top of the dough, Cover with a clean tea towel (dish cloth) and leave to rise in a warm place for about 1 hour, or until doubled in bulk.

3 Meanwhile, make the sauce. Heat oil in a pan, over a medium heat. Add onion and cook for 5 minutes until softened. Add garlic and cook for a few seconds. Add tomatoes, oregano, tomato purée (paste) and season. Bring to the boil and simmer, uncovered, for 30 minutes until thick. Leave to cool.

4 For the seafood, put mussels and clams in a pan with only the water clinging to their shells. Cover and cook over a high heat for 3–4 minutes, shaking occasionally, until the shells have opened. Discard any that remain closed. Strain and discard the cooking liquid. When cool enough to handle, remove the seafood from their shells and set aside.

5 Heat the oil in a frying pan (skillet) and add the prawns (shrimp) and squid. Cook for 2–3 minutes until the prawns have turned pink and the squid has become firm. Do not overcook at this stage.

6 Preheat the oven to 230°C/450°F/Gas Mark 8 with baking sheets (cookie sheet) on the top and middle shelves. Knock back the risen dough and divide in 2 and shape into 25 cm/10 inch in rounds. Put on to floured baking sheets (cookie sheet).

7 Spread half the tomato sauce on each pizza and add the seafood. Season and top with the cheese. Drizzle with olive oil and sit the sheets on top of the preheated sheets. Cook for 12–15 minutes, swapping halfway through the cooking time, until golden. Serve immediately, sprinkled with the basil.

Onion & Tuna Tart

This is a variation of Pissaladiére, the classic French tart of slow-cooked onions on a bread base, very like a pizza.

Serves 4

INGREDIENTS

225 g/8 oz strong white bread flour
1 tsp salt
7 g sachet easy-blend yeast
2 tbsp olive oil
150 ml/5 fl oz/$^{2}/_{3}$ cup hand-hot water

TOPPING:
50 g/1¾ oz/¼ cup butter
2 tbsp olive oil
900 g/2 lb/ 9 oz onions, finely sliced
1 tsp sugar
1 tsp salt
1 tsp fresh thyme leaves
200 g/7 oz can tuna, drained
80 g/3 oz/¼ cup pitted black olives
pepper
green salad, to serve

1 To make the topping, heat the butter and oil in a large saucepan and add the onions. Stir well and cook, covered, over a very low heat for 20 minutes. Add the sugar and salt. Cook, covered, over the lowest heat for a further 30–40 minutes, stirring until collapsed and beginning to brown. Uncover and cook a further 15–10 minutes until evenly golden. Remove from the heat, stir in the thyme and seasoning.

2 Meanwhile, make the base. In a large bowl, mix together the flour, salt and yeast. Add the oil and enough water to make a soft dough that leaves the sides of the bowl clean. Tip the dough on to a lightly floured surface and knead for 5 minutes until smooth and elastic. Alternatively, use a food mixer with a dough hook and knead for 5 minutes.

3 Form the dough into a neat ball and drop into a lightly oiled bowl. Lightly oil the top of the dough, cover with a clean tea towel (dish cloth) and set aside to rise in a warm place for about 1 hour, or until doubled in bulk.

4 Preheat the oven to 220°C/ 450°F/Gas Mark 7 with a baking sheet (cookie sheet) on the top shelf. Knock back the risen dough by punching down the centre with your fist. Tip on to the work surface (counter) and knead briefly. Roll out the dough, using a rolling pin, to fit a lightly oiled Swiss roll tin measuring 32.5 x 23 cm/13 x 9 inches, leaving a rim. You may have to stretch the dough to fit the tin as it is very springy.

5 Spread the onions in an even layer over the dough. Flake the tuna and put on top of the onions. Arrange the olives over the tuna and season with black pepper. Transfer the tin to the preheated baking sheet (cookie sheet) and cook for 20 minutes until the dough is golden. Serve immediately, with a green salad.

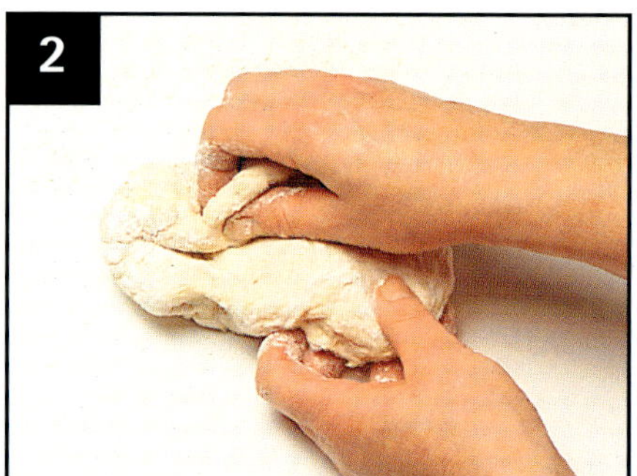

Fish Pasties

This is a seafood variation of a classic Cornish pasty.

Serves 4

INGREDIENTS

450 g/1 lb/4 cups self-raising flour
pinch salt
225 g/8 oz/1¼ cups butter, diced
1 egg, lightly beaten

FILLING:
50 g/1¾ oz/¼ cup butter
80 g/3 oz leek, diced
80 g/3 oz onion, finely chopped
80 g/3 oz carrot, diced
225 g/8 oz potato, diced
350 g/12 oz firm white fish (use the cheapest available), cut into 2.5 cm/1 inch pieces
4 tsp white wine vinegar
25 g/1 oz Cheddar cheese, grated
1 tsp chopped fresh tarragon
salt and pepper

TO SERVE:
mixed salad leaves and tomatoes

1 In a large bowl, sift together the flour and salt. Add the butter and rub in with your fingertips until the mixture resembles coarse breadcrumbs. Add about 3 tablespoons cold water to form a dough. Knead briefly until smooth. Wrap in cling film (plastic wrap) and chill for 30 minutes.

2 To make the filling, melt half the butter in a large frying pan (skillet) and add the leek, onion and carrot. Cook gently for 7–8 minutes until the vegetables are softened. Remove from the heat, put to one side and allow the mixture to cool slightly.

3 Put the vegetable mixture into a large mixing bowl and add the potato, fish, vinegar, remaining butter, cheese, tarragon and seasoning. Set aside.

4 Remove the pastry from the refrigerator and roll out thinly. Using a pastry cutter, press out four 19cm/7½ inch discs. Alternatively, use a small plate of a similar size. Divide the filling between the 4 discs. Moisten the edges of the pastry and fold over. Pinch to seal. Crimp the edges and place the pasties on a lightly greased baking sheet (cookie sheet). Brush generously with the beaten egg, avoiding the base of the pastry to prevent the pasties sticking to it.

5 Bake in a preheated oven at 200°C/400°F/Gas Mark 6 for 15 minutes. Remove from the oven and brush again with the egg glaze. Return to the oven for a further 20 minutes. Serve hot or cold with a salad of mixed leaves and tomatoes.

1

3

4

Buckwheat Pancakes with Smoked Salmon & Crème Fraîche

Buckwheat flour is traditionally used in Breton pancakes. It is available from large supermarkets and health food stores.

Serves 4

INGREDIENTS

55 g/2 oz/½ cup plain (all purpose) flour
55 g/2 oz/½ cup buckwheat flour
pinch salt
2 large eggs
200 ml/7 fl oz/¾ cup milk
85 ml/3 fl oz/scant ½ cup water
25 g/1 oz/2 tbsp butter, melted
vegetable oil for frying

FILLING:
120 ml/4 fl oz/½ cup crème fraîche
1 tbsp capers, drained, rinsed and roughly chopped
3 spring onions (scallions), finely chopped
1 red chilli, deseeded and finely chopped
1 tbsp chopped fresh dill
1 tbsp chopped fresh chives
1 tsp lemon rind
225 g /8 oz sliced smoked salmon
salt and pepper

1 For the filling, mix together the crème fraiche, capers, spring onions (scallions), red chilli, dill, chives, lemon rind and seasoning and set aside.

2 To make the buckwheat pancakes, sift together the flours and salt into a large bowl. Make a well in the centre and add the eggs. Mix together the milk and water and add half this mixture to the flour and eggs. Mix together until smooth. Gradually add the remaining milk until you have a smooth batter. Stir in the melted butter.

3 Heat a 20 cm/8 inch pancake pan or frying pan (skillet) over a medium heat. Dip a piece of wadded paper towel into a little vegetable oil and rub this over the surface of the pan to give a thin coating. Ladle about 2 tablespoons pancake mixture to the pan, tilting and shaking the pan to coat the bottom evenly. Cook for 1 minute until the edges start to lift away from the pan. Using a large palette knife, carefully lift the pancake and turn it over. It should be pale golden. Cook for 30 seconds on the second side. Remove from the pan and place on a warmed plate. Re-grease and reheat the pan and repeat with the remaining mixture to make 12–14 pancakes, depending on their thickness.

4 Place a slice of smoked salmon on each pancake and top with almost 2 teaspoons of the crème fraîche mixture. Fold the pancake in half and then in half again to form a triangle.

Entertaining

The recipes in this chapter have been designed for those occasions when you really want to make an impression. Fish and shellfish are ideal for entertaining.

They are perceived to be more exotic than many meat dishes and yet are often easier to prepare. Shellfish in particular is thought to be luxurious, but nowadays it is readily available and reasonably priced.

There should be something here for every budget, ability and taste, from Stuffed Monkfish Tail and Crab Soufflé to Hot-smoked Trout Tart and Spinach Roulade.

There are more traditional dishes, such as Luxury Fish Pie and Sole Florentine as well as more exciting dishes like Cuttlefish in their own Ink.

Skate with Black Butter

Skate has a strong flavour that makes it a rich fish. It is therefore perfect partnered with this sauce, which is sharp in flavour. I like to serve it with boiled potatoes and a green vegetable.

Serves 4

INGREDIENTS

900 g/2 lb skate wings, cut into 4
175 g/6 oz/¾ cup butter
50 ml/2 fl oz/¾ cup red wine vinegar
15 g/½ oz capers, drained
1 tbsp chopped fresh parsley
salt and pepper

COURT-BOUILLON:
850 ml/1½ pints/3¾ cups cold water
850 ml/1½ pints/3¾ cups dry white wine
3 tbsp white wine vinegar
2 large carrots, roughly chopped
1 onion, roughly chopped
2 celery sticks, roughly chopped
2 leeks, roughly chopped
2 garlic cloves, roughly chopped
2 fresh bay leaves
4 parsley sprigs
4 thyme sprigs
6 black peppercorns
1 tsp salt

TO SERVE:
new potatoes
green vegetable

1 Begin by making the court-bouillon. Put all of the ingredients into a large saucepan and bring slowly to the boil. Cover and simmer gently for 30 minutes. Strain the liquid through a fine sieve into a clean pan. Bring to the boil again and simmer fast, uncovered, for 15–20 minutes, until reduced to 600 ml/1 pint/ 2½ cups.

2 Place the skate in a wide shallow pan and pour over the court-bouillon. Bring to the boil and simmer very gently for 15 minutes, or a little longer depending on the thickness of the skate. Drain the fish and put to one side, keeping warm.

3 Meanwhile, melt the butter in a frying pan (skillet). Cook over a medium heat until the butter changes colour to a dark brown and smells very nutty.

4 Add the vinegar, capers and parsley and allow to simmer for 1 minute. Pour over the fish. Serve immediately with plenty of boiled new potatoes and a any seasonal fresh green vegetable of your choice.

Dover Sole à la Meunière

Dover sole à la Meunière, or 'miller's wife style', gets its name from the light dusting of flour that the fish is given before frying. Seafood chef Rick Stein suggests the addition of a little preserved lemon to give the dish an added piquancy.

Serves 4

INGREDIENTS

- 50 g/1¾ oz/½ cup plain flour
- 1 tsp salt
- 4 x 400 g/14 oz Dover soles, cleaned and skinned
- 150 g/5½ oz/⅔ cup butter
- 3 tbsp lemon juice
- 1 tbsp chopped fresh parsley
- ¼ of a preserved lemon, finely chopped (optional)
- salt and pepper
- lemon wedges, to garnish

1 Mix the flour with the salt and place on a large plate or tray. Drop the fish into the flour, one at a time, and shake well to remove any excess. Melt 40 g/ 1½ oz (3 tablespoons) of the butter in a small saucepan and use to liberally brush the fish all over.

2 Place the fish under a preheated hot grill (broiler) and cook for 5 minutes each side.

3 Meanwhile, melt the remaining butter in pan. Pour cold water into a bowl, large enough to take the base of the pan. Keep nearby.

4 Heat the butter until it turns a golden brown and begins to smell nutty. Remove immediately from the heat and immerse the base of the pan in the cold water, to arrest cooking.

5 Put the fish on to individual serving plates, drizzle with the lemon juice and sprinkle with the parsley and preserved lemon, if using. Pour over the browned butter and serve immediately, garnished with lemon wedges.

COOK'S TIP

If you have a large enough pan (or two) you can fry the floured fish in butter, if you prefer.

1

3

5

Sole Florentine

This is a classic combination of rolled sole fillets in a creamy cheese sauce cooked with spinach. To save time, prepare the cheese sauce in advance.

Serves 4

INGREDIENTS

600 ml/1 pint/$2\frac{1}{2}$ cups milk
2 strips lemon rind
2 sprigs fresh tarragon
1 fresh bay leaf
$\frac{1}{2}$ onion, sliced
50 g/$1\frac{3}{4}$ oz/2 tbsp butter
50 g/$1\frac{3}{4}$ oz /$\frac{1}{2}$ cup plain flour
2 tsp mustard powder
25 g/1 oz/3 tbsp freshly grated Parmesan cheese
300 ml/10 fl oz/$2\frac{1}{4}$ cups double (heavy) cream
pinch freshly grated nutmeg
450 g/1 lb fresh spinach, washed
4 x 750 g/1 lb 10 oz Dover sole, quarter-cut fillets (two from each side of the fish)
salt and pepper

TO SERVE:
crisp green salad
crusty bread

1 Put the milk, lemon rind, tarragon, bay leaf and onion into a saucepan and bring slowly to the boil. Remove from the heat and set aside for 30 minutes for the flavours to infuse.

2 Melt the butter in a clean saucepan and stir in the flour and mustard powder until smooth. Strain the infused milk, discarding the lemon, herbs and onion. Gradually beat the milk into the butter and flour until smooth. Bring slowly to the boil, stirring constantly, until thickened. Simmer gently for 2 minutes. Remove from the heat and stir in the cheese, double (heavy) cream, nutmeg and seasoning. Cover the surface of the sauce with baking parchment or cling film (plastic wrap) and set aside.

2

3 Lightly grease a large baking dish. Blanch the spinach leaves in plenty of boiling salted water for 30 seconds. Drain and immediately refresh under cold water. Drain and pat dry. Put the spinach in a layer on the bottom of the greased dish.

4

4 Wash and dry the fish fillets. Season and roll up. Arrange on top of the spinach and pour over the cheese sauce. Transfer to a preheated oven at 200°C/400°F/ Gas Mark 6 and cook for 35 minutes until bubbling and golden. Serve immediately with a crisp green salad and crusty bread.

VARIATION

For a budget version of this dish, use lemon sole instead of Dover sole.

John Dory en Papillote

The beauty of this dish is that the fish cooks alongside a selection of vegetables, which means you need only cook some boiled new potatoes to serve with it.

Serves 4

INGREDIENTS

- 2 John Dory, filleted
- 115 g/4 oz/1 cup pitted black olives
- 12 cherry tomatoes, halved
- 115 g/4 oz green beans, trimmed
- handful fresh basil leaves
- 4 slices fresh lemon
- 4 tsp olive oil
- salt and pepper
- fresh basil leaves, to garnish
- boiled new potatoes, to serve

1 Wash and dry the fish fillets and set aside. Cut 4 large rectangles of baking parchment measuring about 45 x 30 cm/ 18 x 12 inches. Fold in half to give a 23 x 30 cm/9 x 12 inch rectangle. Cut this into a large heart shape and open out.

2 Lay 1 John Dory fillet on one half of the paper heart. Top with a quarter of the olives, tomatoes, green beans, basil and 1 lemon slice. Drizzle over 1 teaspoon of olive oil and season well with salt and pepper.

3 Fold over the other half of the paper and fold the edges of the paper together to enclose. Repeat to make 4 parcels.

4 Place the parcels on a baking sheet (cookie tray) and cook in a preheated oven at 200°C/400°F/ Gas Mark 6, for 15 minutes or until the fish is tender.

5 Transfer each parcel to a serving plate, unopened, allowing your guests to open their parcels and enjoy the wonderful aroma. Suggest that they garnish their portions with fresh basil and serve with a generous helping of boiled new potatoes.

VARIATIONS

Try spreading the fish with a little olive paste, some chopped sun-dried tomatoes, a little goats' cheese and fresh basil.

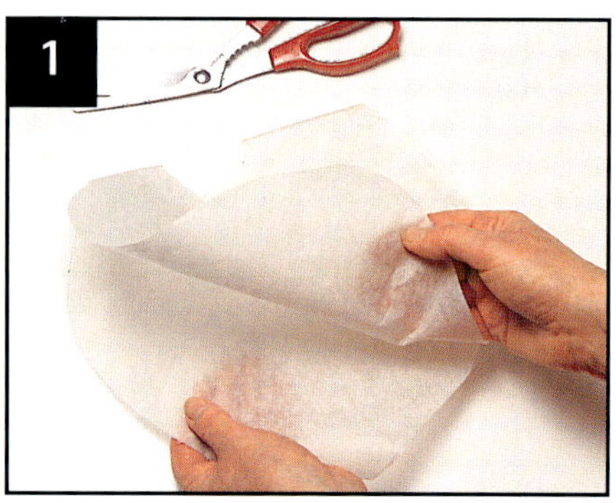
1

2

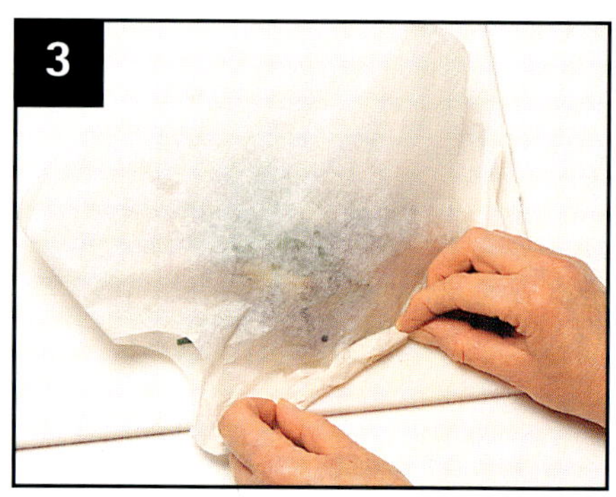
3

Grilled Seabass with Stewed Artichokes

Baby artichokes are slowly cooked with olive oil, garlic, thyme and lemon to create a soft blend of flavours that harmonise very well with the fish, without being overpowering.

Serves 6

INGREDIENTS

1.75 kg/4 lb baby artichokes
$2\frac{1}{2}$ tbsp fresh lemon juice, plus the cut halves of the lemon
150 ml/5 fl oz/$\frac{2}{3}$ cup olive oil
10 garlic cloves, finely sliced
1 tbsp fresh thyme plus extra, to garnish
6 x 115 g/4 oz sea bass fillets
1 tbsp olive oil
salt and pepper
crusty bread, to serve

1 Peel away the tough outer leaves of each artichoke until the yellow-green heart is revealed. Slice off the pointed top at about halfway between the point and the top of the stem. Cut off the stem and pare off what is left of the dark green leaves surrounding the bottom of the artichoke.

2 Submerge the prepared artichokes in water containing the cut halves of the lemon to prevent them browning. When all the artichokes have been prepared, turn them, choke side down, and slice thinly.

3 Warm the olive oil in a large saucepan and add the sliced artichokes, garlic, thyme, lemon juice and seasoning. Cover and cook the artichokes over a low heat for 20–30 minutes, without colouring, until tender.

4 Meanwhile, brush the sea bass fillets with the remaining olive oil and season well. Cook on a preheated ridged grill pan or barbecue for 3–4 minutes on each side until just tender.

5 Divide the stewed artichokes between serving plates and top each with a sea bass fillet. Garnish with chopped thyme and serve with lots of crusty bread.

VARIATIONS

Artichokes cooked this way also suit cod, halibut or salmon.

1

2

4

Sea Bass with Ratatouille

Sea bass is surely the king of round fish, with a delightful flavour and texture. Here it is cooked very simply and served with a highly flavoured sauce of ratatouille and a basil dressing.

Serves 4

INGREDIENTS

2 large sea bass, filleted
olive oil, for brushing
salt and pepper

RATATOUILLE:
1 large aubergine
2 medium courgettes
1 tbsp sea salt
4 tbsp olive oil
1 medium onion, roughly chopped
2 garlic cloves, crushed
½ red (bell) pepper, deseeded and roughly chopped
½ green (bell) pepper, deseeded and roughly chopped
2 large ripe tomatoes, skinned and chopped
1 tbsp freshly chopped basil

DRESSING:
5 tbsp roughly chopped fresh basil
2 garlic cloves, roughly chopped
4 tbsp olive oil
1 tbsp lemon juice
salt and pepper

1 To make the ratatouille, cut the aubergine (eggplant) and courgette (zucchini) into chunks about the same size as the onion and (bell) peppers. Put the aubergine (eggplant) and courgette (zucchini) in a colander with the salt and set aside to drain for 30 minutes. Rinse thoroughly and pat dry on paper towels. Set aside.

2 Heat the oil in a large saucepan and add the onion and garlic. Cook gently for 10 minutes until softened. Add the (bell) peppers, aubergine (eggplant) and courgette (zucchini). Season and stir well. Cover and simmer very gently for 30 minutes until all the vegetables have softened. Add the tomatoes and cook for a further 15 minutes.

1

2

3 Meanwhile make the dressing. Put the basil, garlic, and half the olive oil into a food processor and blend until finely chopped. Add the remaining olive oil, lemon juice and seasoning.

4 Season the sea bass fillets and brush with a little oil. Preheat a frying pan (skillet) until very hot and add the fish, skin side down. Cook for 2–3 minutes until the skin is browned and crispy. Turn the fish and cook for a further 2–3 minutes until just cooked through.

5 To serve, stir the basil into the ratatouille then divide between 4 serving plates. Top with the fresh fried fish and spoon around the dressing.

Whole Seabass with Ginger & Spring Onions (Scallions)

This is a lovely oriental-inspired dish of sea bass, delicately flavoured with spring onions (scallions), ginger and soy sauce. Be careful pouring the hot oil over the fish and spring onions (scallions), as it may spit a little.

Serves 4

INGREDIENTS

800 g/1 lb 12 oz whole sea bass, cleaned and scaled
4 tbsp light soy sauce
5 spring onions (scallions), cut into long, fine shreds
2 tbsp finely shredded fresh ginger root
4 tbsp fresh coriander leaves
5 tsp sunflower oil
1 tsp sesame oil
4 tbsp hot fish stock
steamed rice, to serve
lime wedges, to garnish

1 Wash and dry the fish. Brush with 2 tablespoons of the soy sauce. Scatter half the spring onions (scallions) and all the ginger over a steaming tray or large plate and put the fish on top.

2 Half fill a large saucepan with water and fit a steamer on top. Bring the water to the boil. Put the steaming plate with the sea bass into the steamer and cover with a tight-fitting lid. Keeping the water boiling, steam the fish for 10–12 minutes until tender.

3 Carefully remove the plate and lift the fish on to a serving platter, leaving behind the spring onions and ginger. Scatter over the remaining spring onions (scallions) and coriander leaves.

4 Put the sunflower oil into a small saucepan and heat until almost smoking. Add the sesame oil and immediately pour over the fish and spring onions (scallions). Mix the remaining soy sauce with the fish stock and pour this over the fish. Serve immediately with steamed rice and garnish with lime wedges.

Cold Poached Cod Steaks with a Pickled Vegetable Relish

Poached cod has a very delicate flavour.
Here it is teamed with a piquant relish of finely diced, colourful vegetables, both served cold

Serves 4

INGREDIENTS

1 small carrot, thinly sliced
1 small onion, thinly sliced
1 celery stick, thinly sliced
3 sprigs fresh parsley
3 sprigs fresh thyme
1 garlic clove, sliced
1.75 litres/3 pints/7½ cups water
1 tsp salt
4 x 175 g/6 oz cod steaks

PICKLED VEGETABLE RELISH:
1 small carrot, finely diced
¼ red (bell) pepper, deseeded and finely diced
½ small red onion, finely diced
1 garlic clove, finely chopped
3 tbsp finely diced cornichon pickles
4 tbsp chopped pitted green olives
1 tbsp capers, drained and rinsed
2 salted anchovies, soaked in several changes of water for 15 minutes, chopped
1 tbsp red wine vinegar
100 ml/3½ fl oz/scant ½ cup olive oil
2 tbsp chopped fresh parsley
salt and pepper
salad leaves, to serve

1 Put the carrot, onion, celery, parsley, thyme, garlic, water and salt into a large saucepan. Bring to the boil and simmer gently for 10 minutes. Add the fish and poach for 5–7 minutes until just firm in the centre. Remove the fish with a slotted spoon and leave to cool. Refrigerate for 2 hours.

2 Meanwhile, make the pickled vegetable relish. In a non-metallic bowl, combine the carrot, red (bell) pepper, red onion, garlic, cornichons, olives, capers, anchovies, vinegar, olive oil and parsley. Season to taste, adding a little more vinegar or olive oil to taste. Cover and leave to stand in the refrigerator for 1 hour.

3 To serve, place a cold cod steak on each of 4 serving plates. Spoon the relish over the top. Serve immediately with dressed salad leaves.

Sea Bream in a Salt Crust

Cooking the fish in a layer of salt ensures that the flesh stays very moist without becoming salty.

Serves 4

INGREDIENTS

1 kg/2 lb 4 oz whole sea bream
1 shallot, thinly sliced
2 sprigs fresh parsley
1 sprig fresh tarragon
2 garlic cloves, roughly chopped
2–2.5 kg/4 lb 8 oz–5 lb 8 oz coarse sea salt

LEMON BUTTER SAUCE:
2 shallots, very finely chopped
4 tbsp lemon juice
300 g/10½ oz cold unsalted butter, diced
salt and pepper

TO GARNISH:
lemon wedges
fresh herbs

1 Wash and dry the sea bream. Stuff the body cavity with the shallot, parsley, tarragon and garlic. Set aside.

2 Sprinkle a thick layer of salt into the bottom of a roasting tin (pan) large enough to hold the fish, with lots of space round it. Top with the fish then pour the remaining salt over the fish to completely cover it. Sprinkle the water lightly all over the salt. Cook in a preheated oven for 25 minutes 220°C/425°F/ Gas Mark 7.

3 To make the lemon butter sauce, put the shallots and lemon juice into a saucepan and simmer gently for 5 minutes. Increase the heat until the lemon juice is reduced by half. Reduce the heat and add the butter, piece by piece, whisking constantly, until all the butter is incorporated and the sauce is thick. Season to taste and keep warm.

4 Remove the fish from the oven and allow to stand for 5 minutes before cracking open the salt. Remove the fish, garnish with lemon wedges and fresh herbs and serve with the lemon butter sauce.

COOK'S TIP

Use unscented pure bath salts, if you can find them, rather than the more expensive salt for the table.

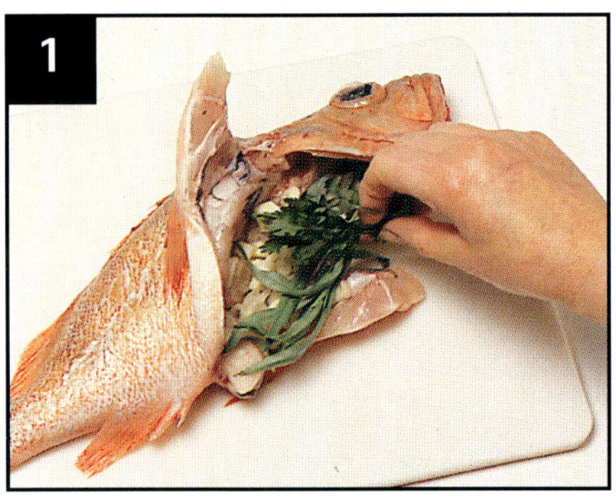
1

2

4

Cuttlefish in their own Ink

This is a dramatic-looking dish due to the inclusion of the cuttlefish ink. Although this is a typically Spanish dish, I have teamed it with polenta as the combination of the dark stew and pale yellow polenta make a beautiful contrast.

Serves 4

INGREDIENTS

- 450 g/1 lb small cuttlefish, with their ink (or substitute squid)
- 4 tbsp olive oil
- 1 small onion, finely chopped
- 2 garlic cloves, finely chopped
- 1 tsp paprika, preferably Spanish
- 175 g/6 oz ripe tomatoes, skinned, deseeded and chopped
- 150 ml/5 fl oz/½ cup red wine
- 150 ml/5 fl oz/½ cup fish stock
- 225 g/8 oz/1½ cups instant polenta
- 3 tbsp chopped fresh flat-leaf parsley
- salt and pepper

1 To prepare the cuttlefish, cut off the tentacles in front of the eyes and remove the beak-like mouth from the centre of the tentacles. Cut the head section from the body and discard it. Cut open the body section from top to bottom along the dark coloured back. Remove the cuttle bone and the entrails, reserving the ink sac. Skin the body. Chop the flesh roughly and set aside. Split open the ink sac and dilute the ink in a little water. Set aside.

2 Heat the oil in a large saucepan and add the onion. Cook gently for 8–10 minutes until softened and starting to brown. Add the garlic and cook for a further 30 seconds. Add the reserved cuttlefish and cook for a further 5 minutes until starting to brown. Add the paprika and stir for a further 30 seconds before adding the tomatoes. Cook for 2–3 minutes until collapsed.

3 Add the red wine, fish stock and diluted ink and stir well. Bring to the boil and simmer gently, uncovered, for 25 minutes until the cuttlefish is tender and the sauce has thickened. Season to taste.

4 Meanwhile, cook the polenta according to the packet instructions. When cooked, remove from the heat and stir in the parsley and seasoning.

5 Divide the polenta between serving plates and top with the cuttlefish and its sauce.

1

2

3

Noisettes of Salmon

This is an interesting and elegant way of presenting an ordinary salmon steak.

Serves 4

INGREDIENTS

4 salmon steaks
50 g/1¾ oz/¼ cup butter, softened
1 garlic clove, crushed
2 tsp mustard seeds
2 tbsp chopped fresh thyme
1 tbsp chopped fresh parsley
2 tbsp vegetable oil
4 tomatoes, skinned, deseeded and chopped
salt and pepper

TO SERVE:
new potatoes
green vegetables or salad

1 Carefully remove the central bone from the salmon steaks and cut them in half. Curl each piece around to form a medallion and tie with string. Blend together the butter, garlic, mustard seeds, thyme, parsley and seasoning and set aside.

2 Heat the oil in a ridged pan or frying pan (skillet) and brown the salmon noisettes on both sides, in batches if necessary. Drain on paper towels and leave to cool.

3 Cut 4 pieces of baking parchment into 30 cm/12 inch squares. Place 2 salmon noisettes on top of each square and top with a little of the flavoured butter and tomato. Draw up the edges of the paper and fold together to enclose the fish. Place on a baking sheet (cookie sheet).

4 Cook in a preheated oven at 200°C/400°F/Gas Mark 6 for 10–15 minutes or until the salmon is cooked through. Serve immediately while still warm with new potatoes and a green vegetable of your choice.

VARIATIONS

You can make cod steaks into noisettes in the same way. Cook them with butter flavoured with chives and basil.

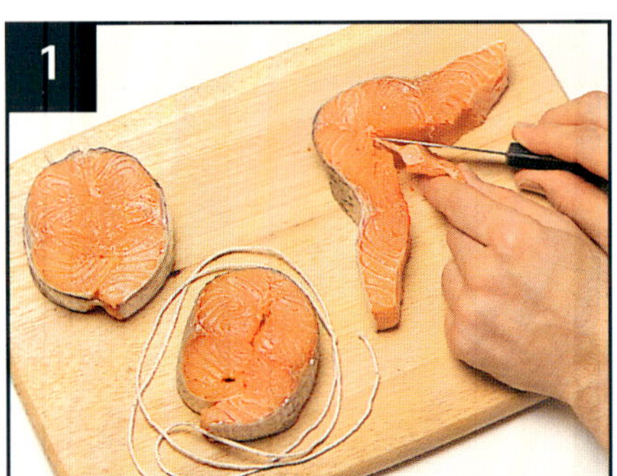

Whole Poached Salmon

Although the fish is quite simply cooked, a whole salmon always makes a very impressive centrepiece.

Serves 4–6

INGREDIENTS

1.5 kg/3 lb 5 oz salmon, cleaned and scaled
3 x quantity court-bouillon (see Poached Rainbow Trout page 122)
½ cucumber, very thinly sliced

WATERCRESS MAYONNAISE:
1 egg yolk
1 garlic clove, crushed
1 tsp Dijon mustard
1 tbsp lemon juice
50 g/1¾ oz watercress leaves, roughly chopped
1 tbsp chopped fresh basil
225 ml/8 fl oz/1 cup light olive oil
1 spring onion (scallion), finely chopped
salt and pepper

1 Wash and dry the salmon and remove the fins. Place the salmon in a fish kettle or large, heavy-based roasting tin (pan). Pour over the court-bouillon. Bring slowly to the boil and as soon as the liquid comes to a simmer, remove from the heat and leave to go cold.

2 Meanwhile, make the watercress mayonnaise. Put the egg yolk, garlic, mustard, lemon juice, watercress and basil into a food processor and blend until the herbs are very finely chopped. Begin adding the olive oil, drop by drop, until the mixture begins to thicken. Continue adding the olive oil in a steady stream until it is all incorporated. Scrape the mayonnaise into a bowl and add the spring onion (scallion) and seasoning. Refrigerate until needed.

3 When the salmon is cold, carefully lift it from the poaching liquid and pat dry. Carefully peel away and discard the skin from the rounder, uppermost side, then carefully turn the fish and remove the skin from the flatter, underside. Carefully slide a large knife along the backbone of the fish to remove the flesh in one piece. Turn it over on to your serving platter so that the cut side is up.

4 Remove the bones from the remaining piece of fish. Finally, turn the remaining flesh on top of the first piece to reform the fish. This makes serving much easier. Place the head and tail back on the fish to make it appear whole.

5 Lay the cucumber slices on top of the fish, starting at the tail end, in a pattern resembling scales. Serve with the mayonnaise.

2

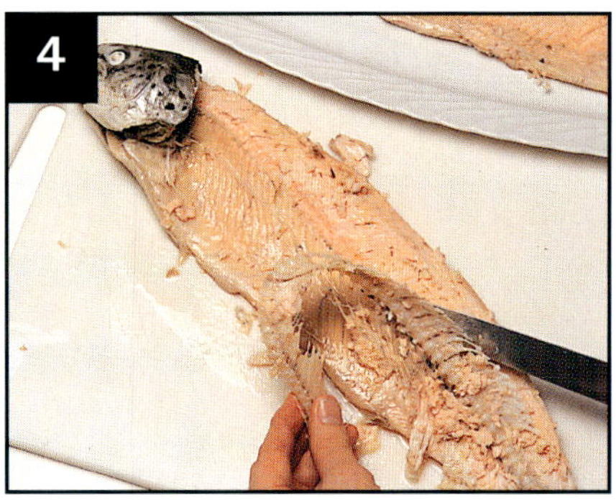

4

Stuffed Monkfish Tail

A very impressive-looking dish which is very simple to prepare.

Serves 6

INGREDIENTS

750 g/1 lb 10 oz monkfish tail, skinned and trimmed
6 slices Parma ham (prosciutto)
4 tbsp chopped mixed herbs such as parsley, chives, basil, sage
1 tsp finely grated lemon rind
2 tbsp olive oil
salt and pepper

TO SERVE:
shredded stir-fried vegetables
new potatoes

1 Using a sharp knife, carefully cut down each side of the central bone of the monkfish to leave 2 fillets. Wash and dry the fillets.

2 Lay the Parma ham (prosciutto) slices widthways on a clean work surface so that they overlap slightly. Lay the fish fillets lengthways on top of the ham so that the two cut sides face each other.

3 Mix together the chopped herbs and lemon rind. Season well. Pack this mixture on to the cut surface of one monkfish fillet. Press the 2 fillets together and wrap tightly with the Parma ham (prosciutto) slices. Secure with string or cocktail sticks (toothpicks).

4 Heat the olive oil in a large ovenproof frying pan (skillet) and place the fish in the pan, seam-side down first, and brown the wrapped monkfish tail all over.

5 Cook in a preheated oven, at 200°C/400°F/Gas Mark 6, for 25 minutes until golden and the fish is tender. Remove from the oven and allow to rest for 10 minutes before slicing thickly. Serve with shredded stir-fried vegetables and new potatoes.

COOK'S TIP

It is possible to remove the central bone from a monkfish tail without separating the two fillets completely. This makes it easier to stuff, but takes some practice.

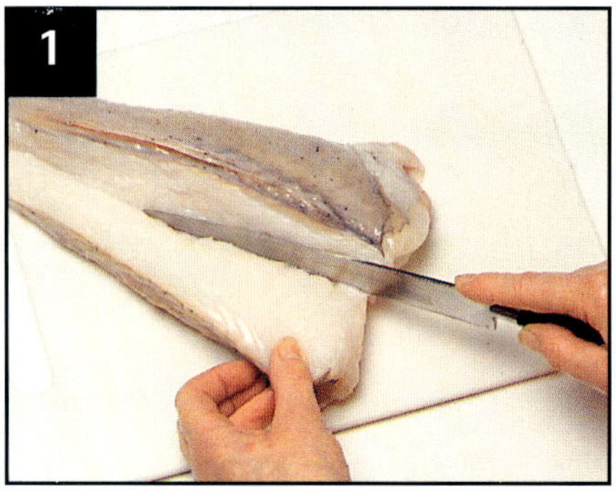

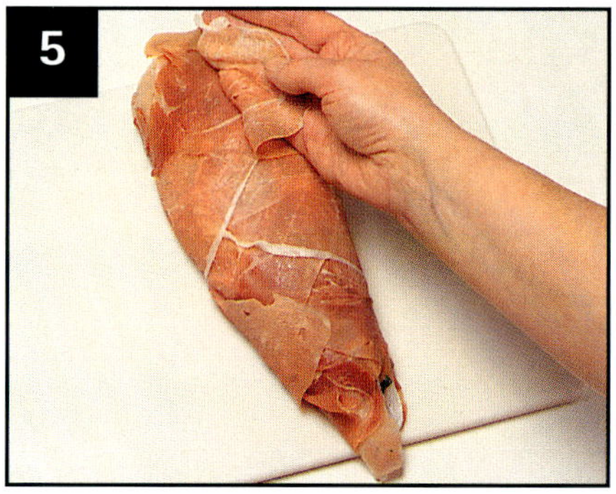

Grilled Lobster with Beurre Blanc

You could cook the lobsters on the barbecue, if you prefer. Cook them shell-side down, to protect the meat from the fierce heat of the fire and cook until nearly cooked then turn briefly flesh-side down.

Serves 4

INGREDIENTS

4 x 450 g/1lb live lobsters
25 g/1 oz/2 tbsp butter

BEURRE BLANC:
25 g/1 oz shallots, finely chopped
1 tbsp white wine vinegar
1 tbsp dry white wine
50 ml/2 fl oz/¼ cup water
150 g/5½ oz/⅔ cup cold unsalted butter, diced
2 tsp chopped fresh tarragon
1 tbsp chopped fresh parsley

TO GARNISH:
salt and pepper
lemon wedges
extra sprigs of fresh herbs

1 Put the lobsters into the freezer for about 2 hours then take a very large knife and cleave them in two, lengthways behind the head. Dot the lobster flesh with the butter. Transfer to a grill (broiler) pan and cook, flesh side up, under a preheated very hot grill (broiler) for 5–7 minutes until the flesh of the lobster becomes firm and opaque.

2 Meanwhile, put the shallots into a small saucepan with the vinegar, white wine and water. Bring to the boil and simmer until only 1 tablespoon of liquid remains. Reduce the heat to low and begin adding the butter, one piece at a time, whisking constantly. Add the next piece of butter when the last bit has been incorporated and continue until you've used all the butter and the sauce has thickened.

3 Stir in the tarragon and parsley and season to taste.

4 Transfer the lobster to 4 serving plates and spoon over the beurre blanc. Garnish with lemon wedges and fresh herbs.

COOK'S TIP

There is controversy about the most humane way to kill a lobster. The RSPCA has suggested that putting the lobsters in a freezer for 2 hours before cooking them will kill them painlessly but, if you are squeamish about such things, you may omit this.

1

3

5

Lobster & Avocado Salad

This isn't really a main course dish but would serve very well as a light lunch with some bread or as part of a buffet.

Serves 4

INGREDIENTS

2 x 400 g/14 oz cooked lobsters
1 large avocado
1 tbsp lemon juice
225 g/8 oz green beans
4 spring onions (scallions), thinly sliced
2 tbsp chopped fresh chervil
1 tbsp chopped fresh chives

DRESSING:
1 garlic clove, crushed
1 tsp Dijon mustard
pinch sugar
1 tbsp balsamic vinegar
5 tbsp olive oil
salt and pepper

1 To prepare the lobsters, cut them in half lengthways. Remove the intestinal vein which runs down the tail, stomach sac and any grey beards from the body cavity at the head end of the lobster. Crack the claws and remove the meat – in one piece if possible. Remove the meat from the tail of the lobster. Roughly chop all the meat and set aside.

2 Split the avocado lengthways and remove the stone. Cut each half in half again and peel away the skin. Cut the avocado into chunks and toss with the lemon juice. Add to the lobster meat.

3 Bring a large pan of salted water to the boil and add the beans. Cook for 3 minutes then drain and immediately refresh under cold water. Drain again and leave to go completely cold. Cut the beans in half then add to the avocado and lobster.

4 Meanwhile, make the dressing by whisking together the garlic, mustard, sugar, vinegar and seasoning. Gradually add the oil, whisking, until thickened.

5 Add the spring onions (scallions), chervil and chives to the lobster and avocado mixture and toss gently together. Drizzle over the dressing and serve immediately.

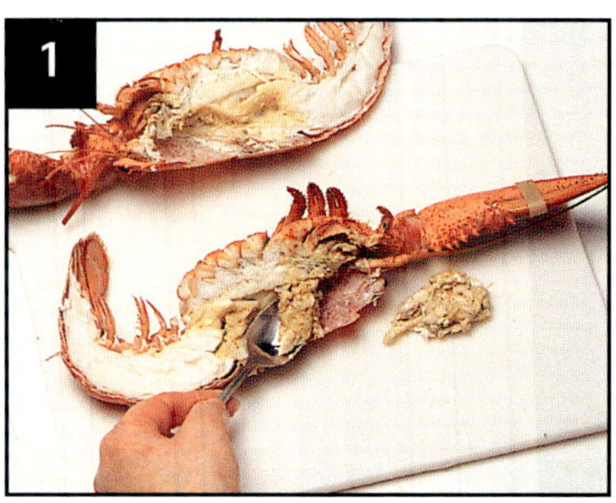
1

3

4

Platter de Fruit de Mers

A platter de fruit de mers is one of the most delightful of all seafood experiences. Use this recipe has a guideline and choose whatever shellfish you find on the day.

Serves 6

INGREDIENTS

36 live mussels, scrubbed and bearded
18 live oysters
3 x 450 g/1 lb cooked lobsters
3 x 750 g/1 lb 10 oz cooked crabs
36 cooked langoustines or prawns
selection of clams, winkles, whelks
cockles, scallops, sea urchins
salt and pepper

MAYONNAISE:
1 egg yolk
1 tsp Dijon mustard
1 tbsp lemon juice
300 ml/10 fl oz/2¼ cups olive oil

SHALLOT VINAIGRETTE:
150 ml/5 fl oz/ ⅔ cup good quality red wine vinegar
3 shallots, finely chopped
1 tbsp olive oil

TO SERVE:
seaweed
crushed ice
3 lemons, cut into wedges

1 To prepare the seafood, steam the mussels, clams and cockles, if using, with just the water on their shells, for 3–4 minutes until just open. Drain and refresh under cold water. If you prefer to serve the oysters lightly cooked (which makes them easier to open), scrub them and put them into a pan with just a splash of water. Cook over a high heat for 3–4 minutes, drain and refresh under cold water. Winkles and whelks need to be boiled in salted water – winkles should be drained as soon as the water returns to a boil and whelks should be simmered for 4 minutes then drained. Scallops should be steamed on the half shell until the flesh just turns white. Sea urchins need only be cut in half and drained of any excess water.

2 To make the mayonnaise, put the egg yolk, mustard, lemon juice and seasoning into a food processor and blend for 30 seconds until foaming. Begin adding the olive oil, drop by drop, until the mixture begins to thicken. Continue adding the olive oil in a steady stream until all the oil is incorporated. Taste for seasoning and add a little hot water if the mixture seems too thick. Refrigerate until needed.

3 For the shallot vinaigrette, mix together the vinegar, shallots, oil and seasoning. Leave at room temperature for 2 hours.

4 To assemble the platter, place the seaweed on a large tray or platter and top with the crushed ice. Arrange the shellfish and crustaceans with the lemon wedges around the platter, scattering on more crushed ice as you go. Serve the mayonnaise and shallot vinaigrette separately.

1

2

Bouillabaisse

As with many traditional French fish stews and soups, the fish and soup are served separately with a strongly flavoured sauce passed around to accompany it.

Serves 6–8

INGREDIENTS

5 tbsp olive oil
2 large onions, finely chopped
1 leek, finely chopped
4 garlic cloves, crushed
½ small fennel bulb, finely chopped
5 ripe tomatoes, skinned and chopped
1 sprig fresh thyme
2 strips orange rind
1.75 litres/3 pints/6½ cups hot fish stock

2 kg/4 lb 8oz mixed fish, such as John Dory, sea bass, bream, red mullet, cod, skate, soft shell crabs, raw prawns, langoustines, roughly chopped into equal-sized pieces (shellfish left whole)
12–18 thick slices French bread
salt and pepper

RED (BELL) PEPPER AND SAFFRON SAUCE:
1 red (bell) pepper, deseeded and quartered
150 ml/5 fl oz/⅔ cup light olive oil
1 egg yolk
large pinch saffron
pinch chilli flakes
lemon juice, to taste

1 To begin, make the red (bell) pepper and saffron sauce. Brush the red pepper quarters with a little of the olive oil. Place under a preheated hot grill (broiler), cook for 5–6 minutes on each side until charred and tender. Remove from the heat and place in a plastic bag until cool enough to handle. Peel the skins away .

2 Place the pepper pieces into a food processor with the egg yolk, saffron, chilli flakes, lemon juice and seasoning and process until smooth. Begin adding the remaining olive oil, drop by drop, until the mixture begins to thicken. Continue adding the olive oil in a steady stream until it is all incorporated and the mixture is thick. Add a little hot water if it seems too thick.

3 In a large pan, heat the olive oil, add the onions, leek, garlic and fennel and cook for 10–15 minutes until softened and start-ing to colour. Add the tomatoes, thyme, orange rind and seasoning and fry for a further 5 minutes until the tomatoes have collapsed.

4 Add the fish stock and bring to the boil. Simmer gently for 10 minutes until all the vegetables are tender. Add the fish and return to the boil. Simmer gently for 10 minutes until all the fish is tender.

5 When the soup is ready, toast the bread on both sides. Using a slotted spoon, divide the fish between serving plates. Add some of the soup to moisten the stew and serve with the bread. Pass around the red (bell) pepper and saffron sauce to accompany. Serve the remaining soup separately.

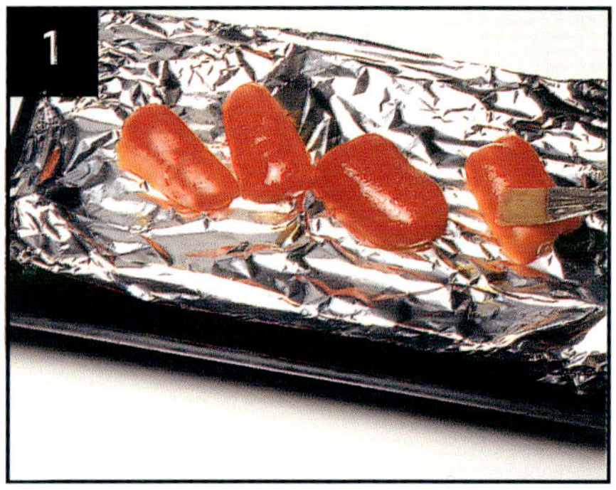

Crab Soufflé

Soufflés are always impressive and this one is no exception. Serve straight from the oven but don't worry if it sinks en route to the table – it's the nature of the beast.

Serves 4–6

INGREDIENTS

40 g/1½ oz/¼ cup plus 1 tbsp butter, plus extra for greasing
25 g/1 oz dried breadcrumbs
1 small onion, finely chopped
1 garlic clove, crushed
2 tsp mustard powder
25 g/1 oz/¼ cup plain flour
225 ml/8 fl oz/1 cup milk
50 g/1¾ oz Gruyère cheese, grated
3 eggs, separated
225 g/8 oz fresh crab meat, thawed if frozen
2 tbsp chopped fresh chives
pinch cayenne
salt and pepper

1 Generously butter a 1.15 litre/2½ pint soufflé dish. Add the breadcrumbs and shake around the dish to coat completely, shaking out any excess. Set aside on a baking sheet (cookie sheet).

2 Melt the butter in a large saucepan. Add onion and cook gently for 8 minutes until softened but not coloured. Add the garlic and cook for a further minute. Add the mustard powder and flour and cook for 1 minute. Gradually add the milk, stirring constantly, until smooth. Increase the heat slightly and bring slowly to the boil, stirring constantly. Simmer gently for 2 minutes. Remove from the heat and stir in the cheese. Leave to cool slightly.

3 Lightly beat in the egg yolks then fold in the crab meat, chives, cayenne and season generously.

4 In a clean bowl, whisk the egg whites until they hold stiff peaks. Add a large spoonful of the egg whites to the crab mixture and fold together to slacken. Add the remaining egg whites and fold together carefully but thoroughly. Spoon into the prepared dish.

5 Cook in a preheated oven at 200°C/400°F/Gas Mark 6 for 25 minutes until well risen and golden. Serve immediately.

2

3

4

Spinach Roulade

This is very nice served with the Quick Tomato Sauce that accompanies the Tuna Fishcakes on page 142.

Serves 4

INGREDIENTS

225 g/8 oz frozen spinach, thawed and well-drained
25 g/1 oz/2 tbsp butter
25 g/1 oz/¼ cup plain flour
200 ml/7 fl oz/¾ cup milk
4 eggs, separated
1 tbsp chopped fresh tarragon
½ tsp freshly grated nutmeg
olive oil for brushing
salt and pepper

FILLING:
375 g/12 oz skinless smoked cod fillet
125 g/4 oz ricotta cheese
25 g/1 oz Parmesan cheese, grated
4 spring onions (scallions), finely chopped
2 tbsp freshly chopped chives
50 g/1¾ oz sun-dried tomatoes in olive oil, drained and finely chopped

1 Grease a 33 x 23 cm/13 x 9 inch Swiss roll tin and line with baking parchment. Squeeze the spinach to remove as much liquid as possible. Chop finely and set aside.

2 Melt the butter in a saucepan, add the flour and cook for 30 seconds, stirring. Gradually add the milk until smooth, stirring constantly. Bring slowly to the boil and simmer for 2 minutes, stirring. Remove from the heat and allow to cool slightly.

3 Stir in the spinach, egg yolks, tarragon, nutmeg and seasoning. Whisk the egg whites until they hold stiff peaks. Fold a large spoonful into the spinach mixture to slacken it then fold in the remaining egg whites, carefully but thoroughly to avoid losing any volume. Pour the mixture into the prepared tin and smooth the surface.

3

5

4 Cook in a preheated oven at 200°C/400°F/Gas Mark 6, for 15 minutes until risen and golden and firm in the centre. Turn out immediately on to a clean tea towel (dish cloth), peel off the baking parchment and roll up from one short end.

5 For the filling, cover the fillet with boiling water and leave for 10 minutes until just tender. Remove the fish and flake carefully, removing any bones, and mix with the ricotta, Parmesan, spring onions (scallions), chives, sun-dried tomatoes and seasoning.

6 Unroll the roulade and spread with the cod mixture, leaving a 2.5 cm/1 inch border all around. Tightly re-roll the roulade and return to the oven, seam side down, for 20 minutes.

Luxury Fish Pie

This is a fish pie for pushing out the boat!

Serves 4

INGREDIENTS

80 g/3 oz/½ cup butter
3 shallots, finely chopped
115 g/4 oz/2 cups button mushrooms, halved
2 tbsp dry white wine
900 g/2 lb live mussels, scrubbed and bearded
1 quantity court-bouillon (see Poached Rainbow Trout, page 122)
300 g/10½ oz monkfish fillet, cubed
300 g/10½ oz skinless cod fillet, cubed
300 g/10½ oz skinless lemon sole fillet, cubed
115 g/4 oz tiger prawns (jumbo shrimp), peeled
25 g/1 oz/¼ cup plain (all purpose) flour
50 ml/2 fl oz/¼ cup double (heavy) cream

POTATO TOPPING:
1.5 kg/3 lb 5oz floury potatoes, cut into chunks
50 g/1¾ oz/¼ cup butter
2 egg yolks
120 ml/4 fl oz/½ cup milk
pinch freshly grated nutmeg
salt and pepper
fresh parsley, to garnish

1 For the filling, melt 25 g/1 oz of the butter in a frying pan (skillet), add the shallots and cook for 5 minutes until softened. Add the mushrooms and cook over a high heat for 2 minutes. Add the wine and simmer until the liquid has evaporated. Transfer to a 1.5 litre/2¾ pint/6¼ cup shallow ovenproof dish and set aside.

2 Put the mussels into a large saucepan with just the water clinging to their shells and cook, covered, over a high heat for 3–4 minutes until all the mussels have opened. Discard any that remain closed. Drain, reserving the cooking liquid. When cool enough to handle, remove the mussels from their shells and add to the mushrooms.

3 Bring the court-bouillon to the boil and add the monkfish. Poach gently for 2 minutes before adding the cod, sole and prawns (shrimp). Poach a further 2 minutes. Remove the fish with a slotted spoon and add to the mussels and mushrooms.

4 Melt the remaining butter in a saucepan and add the flour. Stir until smooth and cook for 2 minutes without colouring. Gradually, stir in the hot court-bouillon and mussel cooking liquid until smooth and thickened. Add the cream and simmer gently for 15 minutes, stirring. Season to taste and pour over the fish.

5 Meanwhile, make the topping. Boil the potatoes in plenty of salted water for 15–20 minutes until tender. Drain well and mash with the butter, egg yolks, milk, nutmeg and seasoning. Pipe over the fish, or spread with a spatula, and roughen the surface of the topping with a fork.

6 Bake the finished fish pie in a preheated oven at 200°C/400°F/Gas Mark 6, for 30 minutes until golden and bubbling. Serve straight from the oven, piping hot with a garnish of fresh parsley.

Salmon Coulibiac

This dish originated in Russia and traditionally used buckwheat in place of rice. The original versions were much larger and needed more than one person to carry them to the table.

Serves 4

INGREDIENTS

50 g/1¾ oz/⅓ cup long grain rice
pinch salt
3 eggs
2 tbsp vegetable oil
1 onion, finely chopped
1 garlic clove, crushed
1 tsp finely grated lemon rind
2 tbsp chopped fresh parsley
1 tbsp chopped fresh dill
450 g/1 lb salmon fillet, skinned and cubed
500 g/1 lb 2 oz puff pastry
beaten egg, to glaze

QUICK HOLLANDAISE SAUCE:
175 g/6 oz/¾ cup butter
1 tbsp wine vinegar
2 tbsp lemon juice
3 egg yolks
salt and pepper

1 Cook the rice with the pinch of salt in plenty of boiling water for 7–8 minutes until tender. Drain well and set aside. Bring a small saucepan of water to the boil and add the eggs. Cook for 8 minutes from when the water returns to the boil. Drain and refresh under cold water. When cool enough to handle, shell and slice thinly.

2 Heat the oil in a frying pan(skillet) and add the onion. Cook gently for 5 minutes until softened. Add the garlic and cook for a further 30 seconds. Add to the rice with the lemon rind, parsley, dill and salmon.

3 Roll out pastry to a rectangle measuring 40 x 30 cm/16 x 12 inches). Lift pastry on to a lightly baking sheet (cookie sheet). Spoon half the filling onto one half of the pastry, leaving a border about 2 cm ¾ inch. Top with the sliced eggs, then the remaining filling.

4 Dampen the outside edges of the pastry with a little beaten egg then fold over the remaining pastry. Crimp the edges to seal well. Mark the pastry using a small sharp knife, taking care not to cut through the pastry. Decorate with pastry trimmings and brush with beaten egg.

5 Bake in a preheated oven at 200°C/400°F/Gas Mark 6 for 30–35 minutes until is risen and golden.

6 For the sauce, put the butter into a small saucepan and melt slowly. Put the wine vinegar and lemon juice into another saucepan and bring to the boil. Meanwhile, put the egg yolks and a pinch of salt in a food processor or blender and blend together. With the motor still running, gradually add the hot vinegar and lemon juice. When the butter starts to boil, start to pour this into the machine in a steady stream until all the butter has been added and the sauce has thickened. Season.

7 Keep warm by placing in a bowl over hot water. Serve the pie with a little hollandaise sauce.

Salmon & Courgette (Zucchini) Pie

This pie is simplicity itself and can be prepared ahead and reheated just before serving.

Serves 4

INGREDIENTS

2 tbsp olive oil
2 red (bell) peppers, cored, deseeded and chopped
1 medium onion, finely chopped
2 eggs
225 g/8 oz salmon fillet, skinned and cubed
1 courgette (zucchini), sliced
1 tsp chopped fresh dill
salt and pepper
Chinese garlic, to garnish

PASTRY:
350 g/12 oz/3 cups plain (all purpose) flour
½ tsp salt
175 g/6 oz/¾ cup cold butter, diced
2 egg yolks
beaten egg or milk, to glaze

1 Heat the oil in a saucepan, add the (bell) peppers, onion and a little seasoning and cook gently for 10–15 minutes, until softened. Transfer to a food processor or blender and blend until smooth or press through a fine sieve.

2 Bring a small saucepan of water to the boil. Add the eggs, cook for 10 minutes from when the water returns to the boil then refresh immediately under cold water. When cool enough to handle, drain and shell.

3 Roughly chop the eggs and add to the pepper purée with the salmon, courgette (zucchini), dill and seasoning. Mix well and set aside.

4 For the pastry, put the flour in a bowl with ½ teaspoon salt. Add the butter and rub in with your fingertips until the mixture resembles fine breadcrumbs. Add the egg yolks with enough cold water, about 3–4 tablespoons, to make a firm dough. Turn on to a lightly floured work surface (counter) and knead briefly until the dough is smooth.

5 Roll out a little over half of the dough and use to line a 23 cm/9 inch pie plate. Fill with the salmon mixture and dampen the edges with a little water. Roll out the remaining pastry and use to cover the pie, pinching the edges to seal. Make a cross or slash in the top of the pie for steam to escape. Re-roll any pastry trimmings and cut into fish tails or leaf shapes and use to decorate the edges of the pie, attaching them with a little beaten egg or milk. Brush more egg or milk over the rest of the pie to glaze.

6 Bake in a preheated oven at 200°C/400°F/Gas Mark 6 for 35–40 minutes until the pastry is golden. Serve hot and garnish with Chinese garlic.

Hot-smoked Trout Tart

Hot-smoked trout is available from fishmongers and large supermarkets. The fish is smoked in a hot environment, which cooks the flesh as well as flavouring it.

Serves 6

INGREDIENTS

175 g/6 oz/1½ cups plain (all purpose) flour
1 tsp salt
80 g/3 oz/⅓ cup butter, cut into small pieces
1 egg yolk

FILLING:
25 g/1 oz/2 tbsp butter
1 small onion, finely chopped
1 tsp green peppercorns in brine, drained and roughly chopped
2 tsp stem (candied) ginger, drained
2 tsp stem (candied) ginger syrup
225 g/8 oz hot-smoked trout fillets, flaked
3 egg yolks
100 ml/3½ fl oz/ scant ½ cup crème fraîche
100 ml/3½ fl oz/ scant ½ cup double (heavy) cream
1 tbsp chopped fresh parsley
1 tbsp chopped fresh chives
salt and pepper

1 Sift together the flour and salt. Add the butter and rub in well with your fingertips until the mixture resembles coarse breadcrumbs. Add the egg yolk and about 2 tablespoons cold water, to make a firm dough. Knead briefly, wrap in cling film (plastic wrap) and refrigerate for 30 minutes.

2 Meanwhile, make the filling. Melt the butter in a frying pan (skillet) and add the onion. Cook gently for 8–10 minutes until softened but not coloured. Remove from the heat and stir in the peppercorns, ginger, ginger syrup and flaked trout. Set aside.

3 Remove the pastry from the refrigerator and roll out thinly. Use to line a 23 cm/9 inch flan tin or dish. Prick the base at regular intervals with a fork. Line the pastry with foil or baking parchment and baking beans. Bake in a preheated oven at 200°C/ 400°F/Gas Mark 6 for 12 minutes. Remove the foil or baking parchment and beans and bake for a further 10 minutes until light golden and dry. Remove from the oven and allow to cool slightly. Reduce the oven temperature to 180°C/350°F/Gas Mark 4. Spread the trout mixture over the base of the pastry.

4 Mix together the egg yolks, crème fraîche, cream, parsley, chives and seasoning. Pour this mixture over the trout mixture to cover. Bake in the preheated oven for 35–40 minutes until just set and golden. Remove from the oven and allow to cool slightly before serving with a mixed green salad or green vegetable.

2

3

Smoked Haddock & Spinach Tart

Smoked haddock gives this easy tart a deliciously savoury flavour.

Serves 6

INGREDIENTS

80 g/3 oz/⅔ cup wholemeal (whole wheat) flour
80 g/3 oz/⅔ cup plain (all purpose) flour
pinch salt
80 g/3 oz/½ cup chilled butter, diced

FILLING:
350 g/12 oz smoked haddock fillet
150 ml/5 fl oz/⅔ cup plus 2 tbsp milk
150 ml/5 fl oz/⅔ cup plus 2 tbsp double (heavy) cream
115 g/4 oz frozen leaf spinach, thawed
3 egg yolks, lightly beaten
80 g/3 oz mature Cheddar cheese, grated
salt and pepper

TO SERVE:
chicary (endive)
watercress leaves
orange, segments

1 For the pastry, mix the two flours together in a bowl with the salt. Add the butter and rub in with your fingertips until the mixture resembles fine breadcrumbs. Stir in enough cold water, about 2–3 tablespoons, to make a firm dough. Knead the pastry briefly until the surface is smooth.

2 Roll out the dough thinly and use to line a 20 cm/8 inch deep fluted flan tin (pan). Put the lined tin (pan) in the freezer for 15 minutes. Line with foil or baking parchment and baking beans and place in a preheated oven, at 200°C/ 400°F/Gas Mark 6, for 10–12 minutes. Remove the foil or parchment and beans and bake for a further 10 minutes until pale golden and dry. Cool slightly. Reduce oven temperature to 190°C/375°F/Gas Mark 5.

3 For the filling, place the haddock in a frying pan (skillet), cover with milk and cream. Bring to the boil, cover and remove from heat. Leave for 10 minutes until the haddock is tender. Remove the fish using a slotted spoon. Strain the cooking liquid into a jug. Skin and flake the fish.

4 Press the spinach in a sieve or squeeze well to remove excess liquid. Arrange the spinach in the the pastry case with the flaked fish. Add the egg yolks to the fish poaching liquid along with 55 g/2 oz of the cheese and seasoning. Mix and pour into the pastry case. Sprinkle over the remaining cheese and bake for 25–30 minutes until the filling is risen, golden and just set.

Index